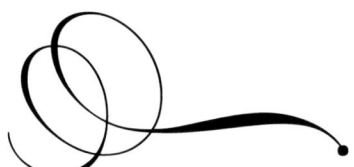

Copyright © 2015 Passager Books
All rights reserved
First Edition 2015
Published in the United States of America
Printed by Spencer Printing

Publisher's Cataloging-In-Publication Data
(Prepared by The Donohue Group, Inc.)

View from the hilltop : a collection by The North Oaks Writers / edited by Barbara Roswell & Christine Drawl. -- First edition.

   pages : illustrations ; cm

   Summary: "A collection of personal essays and poems by members of the North Oaks Retirement Community writing group, located in Pikesville, Maryland."--Provided by publisher.
   ISBN: 978-0-9836209-9-0

   1. Older people--Literary collections. 2. Older people's writings, American--Maryland--Pikesville. 3. Poetry. 4. Essays. I. Roswell, Barbara Sherr, 1959- II. Drawl, Christine. III. North Oaks Writers (Organization)

PS508.A44 V54 2015
810.809285

Cover Art and Design by Pantea Amin Tofangchi
Passager Books is in residence in the Klein Family School of Communications Design at the University of Baltimore.

Passager Books
1420 North Charles Street
Baltimore, Maryland 21201
www.passagerbooks.com

View from the Hilltop

A Collection by The North Oaks Writers
Edited by Barbara Sherr Roswell & Christine Drawl

Passager Books
Baltimore, MD
2015

Foreword

 For the last several years, Barbara Roswell has conducted a writing group for North Oaks residents. The topics have varied from session to session, allowing residents to explore their creativity, develop their writing skills as a form of expression, and in some instances, find catharsis.

 Over the past 25 years, North Oaks has offered its residents a wide variety of artistic, creative, intellectual and cultural opportunities for learning, growth, expression and diversion. It is quite fitting that we present this collection of works by the North Oaks Writers as part of our 25th Anniversary celebration. We hope you will enjoy reading our residents' work.

 We wish to express our deep gratitude to Barbara Roswell not only for leading the writing group over the years, but also for her inspiration to create this volume and her dedicated efforts to bring it to fruition.

Mark Pressman
Executive Director
North Oaks 2015

Arrival

33 **Outside My Window**
Beverly Share

34 **A Change**
Joshua Roseman

35 **Letting Go**
Margie Warres

37 **Retirement Uncorked**
Joshua Roseman

38 **Decoding North Oaks**
Marty Waxman

39 **A Peek**
Mike Roseman

40 **A Pest**
Lee Rubin

41 **Every Evening and Once A Week**
Marty Waxman

44 **The Wye Oak**
Hilda Perl Goodwin

Innocence

49   **The First Kiss**
Carol Suplicki

50   **A Good Choice**
Lorraine Gelula

51   **Vice President Nixon**
Margie Warres

52   **The Bayonet**
Mike Roseman

53   **Playing War**
Carol Suplicki

54   **The First Time I Set A House On Fire**
Mike Roseman

56   **A Memorable Day**
Hilda Perl Goodwin

58   **Graduation, June 1943**
Mike Roseman

59   **The Back Seat**
Margie Warres

62   **Ode to a Spider**
Beverly Share

Defiance

65 The Eight-Second Hero
Howard J. Cohen

68 A Story I Don't Want to Tell
Mike Roseman

70 History Lesson
Howard J. Cohen

74 Glory
Edith Sherr

75 Report Card
Hilde Gundel

76 I Don't Give a Fig
Beverly Share

77 Trees
Marty Waxman

78 Vengeance
Carol Suplicki

Doubt

81   **Things I Do Not Understand**
Beverly Share

82   **A Psalm over the Pacific**
Howard J. Cohen

84   **Why I Gave Up My Childhood Dream**
Marty Waxman

86   **My Obituary**
Beverly Share

87   **Wishing**
Edith Sherr

90   **God and I**
The Writing Group

92   **If**
Hilda Perl Goodwin

Release

95 **Good to Be Out**
Beverly Share

96 **Sixteen**
Edith Sherr

97 **Home from Korea**
Howard J. Cohen

99 **No Heat**
Edith Sherr

102 **I Never Met**
Beverly Share

103 **Uncle Louie and the Comic**
Marty Waxman

104 **Every Meal a Banquet**
Marty Waxman

106 **Breakfast in September, 1941**
Hilde Gundel

Legacy

109   **Before North Oaks**
Carol Suplicki

110   **Evening Meal**
Carol Suplicki

114   **The Shoe and the Grove**
Mike Roseman

116   **Proof of Living**
Eva Slonitz

120   **To Anne**
Joshua Roseman

Redefinition

123   **A Perfect Day**
Lorraine Gelula

124   **In My Dreams**
Beverly Share

126   **You Never Wrote Me a Shakespearean Verse**
Carol Suplicki

127   **A New Decree**
Joshua Roseman

129   **Pomp and Circumstance**
Lorraine Gelula

130   **The Ideal Music Shop**
Hilda Perl Goodwin

132   **Following Edward Roseman**
Mike Roseman

136   **Ode to My Dad's Violin**
Margie Warres

138   **A Sense of Gratitude**
Margie Warres

139 **Courage**
Margie Warres

140 **On My Way to Tomorrow**
Judy Michelson

141 **The Top of the Stairway**
The Writing Group

142 **Depends on What the Weather Brings**
Carol Suplicki

View from the Hilltop

Introduction

When you teach writing at North Oaks, you are in the company of virtuosi musicians. They have been playing their instruments long enough rarely to need practice. Every other Wednesday, at 10:30 a.m., they assemble. One takes out a treasured Strad, long sitting in a dusty attic. Another prepares his French horn, bright and brassy, and you must remind him that the piece calls for *piano*, not *forte*. A third must be coaxed to assemble her flute; you remind her that the best way to warm her fingers is by playing. The musicians look to you for dynamics and tempo, but, really, your job is just to call everyone to attention. You tune. Then you listen to the resplendent solos, the ensemble, the harmonies and echoes, the stirring symphonies the musicians play.

The workshop is a shiny paperweight you hold in your hands. It's your job to shake it — gently — and make it sparkle for an hour. Each week, a different image appears: skaters holding hands on a snowy lake, confetti and streamers flying through the air at a V-E day parade, the grainy image of man's first steps on the moon, the devastation of the Twin Towers falling.

The North Oaks writers take you traveling through memory's winding basement corridors, carousing with rhyming couplets, soaring over vast distances with just words beneath the wings. You meander down the streets of Baltimore City in the 1920s to the Ideal Music Shop, absorb the shock of Pearl Harbor, camp on Korean battlefields, meet Jackie Mason, celebrate marriages and careers, ride horseback in Afghanistan. You debate Donald Trump and share hard won advice for great-grandchildren whose lives are just beginning.

Together, the writing workshop preserves stories and memories. But no frogs in formaldehyde here. Preserving memories is more like a communal jam making project. We harvest and hull and lick the juice from our fingers. The room fills with sweet aromas. Some weeks the jars are brightly colored, filled with deep reds and purples. Over time we experiment with more exotic recipes: pale peach, flecked with rosemary or ginger. We craft and revise. This time the jam is sweet, but it has a kick.

Thus, the writing workshop is more than a collection of individual writers, the whole greater than the sum of the parts. Much of the pleasure is in the nods of recognition, murmurs of appreciation, and knowing exchanges that change the quality of the air in the room, sometimes leaving us breathless. The workshop is like a congregation, the minyan in Jewish tradition that elevates and amplifies individual prayer.

Our process is simple. Usually, I open with a prompt, a fishing line we cast into the water. We write, trusting that the language will reel in a memory or insight lingering in the depths. Often enough, it's a big one, shimmering with flashes of color.

Someone volunteers to read her work aloud. She tosses out some words, a ball of twine we pass back and forth, weaving a web of associations, an entire fabric of connections, wise or amusing. One cold morning last May I asked, *What two things never come soon enough?* We each wrote for a moment, then shared: *Springtime and wisdom. Children and grandchildren.*

Understanding and forgiveness. The elevator and the mail. This book holds a few of these choral pieces, shared reflections that showcase the diverse perspectives generated around the table.

More often writers begin a longer piece, and then use the group's feedback to revise for the next session. Over the years, the group has written about memorable meals and favorite songs, courage and loss, celebrity and politics, first times and last times. They've written sonnets, essays, haiku, speeches, dialogues, and ditties. The workshop acts like a kiln: the writing transforms what at first looks faded and dull, bringing to life the color and gloss and texture.

And it is good, in the words of Socrates, that we should ask the old who have been along a road we all must travel the nature of that road. More than half of today's 74 million baby boomers will likely live past 85. Americans are living on average 34 years longer today than our great-grandparents did – an entire second adult lifetime that's been added to our lifespan. I've learned much.

At some moments, I'm the awkward bystander in the room, not quite catching the music everyone else hears in the background. The North Oaks writers share many worlds, from intimate touchstones – the clever lines of a Danny Kaye song, the charm of Mary Anne, the beloved first elephant to live at the Baltimore Zoo – to the Greatest Generation values of duty, honor and faith forged in an era of Depression and War. In Tom Brokaw's words, It is a generation of towering achievement and modest demeanor that, made few "demands of homage from those who followed and prospered because of its sacrifices." In my experience, the North Oaks writers are modest, indeed, awed by *their* parents' achievements, and seeing themselves as simply doing for their own families what their parents did for them. Every day, I am inspired by their quiet gusto, soft fortitude, pliant determination.

I am also glad for the excuse this collection gave me to visit each writer's apartment. You would not know from North Oaks' stylish burnt umber hallways how varied and distinctive the home each resident has created. Some overflow with souvenirs accumulated through a lifetime of travel, some are delicate and floral, some all desk and bookcase and business. In many you'll be greeted by photos of grandparents born before the Civil War, their warmth visible in the smile that belies their starched, sepia poses. In one, a table filled with newly completed watercolors, another with Resident Association memos and bylaw changes, another with cards received and mail to be sent. Many apartments are hotbeds of activity.

This collection celebrates the convergence of two milestones: the 25th anniversary of North Oaks, and the 25th anniversary of *Passager*. Edited by Mary Azrael and Kendra Kopelke, *Passager* was founded to create beautiful publications that would to bring attention to older writers and encourage the imagination throughout our lives. Under Managing Editor Christine Drawl's direction, and with the wave of Art Director Pantea Amin Tofangchi's magical wand, the *Passager* team has achieved this once again, and with extraordinary grace.

The shape of the book – from *Arrival* and *Innocence*, through *Defiance* and *Doubt*, reaching *Release*, *Legacy* and *Redefinition* – is thanks to Co-Editor Christine Drawl's vision, sensitivity and determination to transform a decade of work by a dozen seniors into one collection that moves dramatically from the first page to the last. As a group, we have come to see age not as an arc, peaking in middle age and then descending into decline, but as a staircase, with each decade, indeed each day, as a step up to new wisdom and vision. You'll see that this book mirrors this contour of ongoing ascent. It includes dramatic steps forward, glimpses backward, and lots of appreciation for fellow travelers and guiding along the way.

Christine Drawl immersed herself in the writers' work, sifting through towering stacks of handwritten pages, some in perfect teacher penmanship, some scrawled hastily on the back of last week's Oak Room menu, some saved in a red Macy's sweater box. She typed up drafts, and then listened for music, nuance and image, bringing the experiences on the pages to life, even visiting addresses mentioned in the stories. With her talented and generous *Passager* colleagues Kendra Kopelke, Mary Azrael and Pantea Amin Tofangchi, she identified themes and relationships, fostered a conversation among the essays that approximates the conversation in the room, and brought the spirit of the workshop to life in these pages.

This project is the work of many hands at North Oaks as well. We thank the staff for readying the seventh floor for us; Activity Coordinator Sherrie Polsky for scheduling our meetings while expertly balancing the many other workshops, lectures, trips and events that North Oaks sponsors; Betty Jontiff and Brenda Lerner for support and encouragement; workshop participant Edith Sherr for serving as liaison, secretary, amanuensis and muse; and Mark Pressman, distinguished, much respected, and well-loved Executive Director of North Oaks, for sharing the ambitious vision for this project and making it possible.

• BARBARA SHERR ROSWELL

Welcome
from the North Oaks Writers
. . . you don't have to drive home.

Welcome to the North Oaks Writers. We're glad to have you join us. We may not be the Algonquin Round Table, that famous group of 30 writers, editors, publicists and actors who met periodically at New York's Algonquin Hotel in the Roaring 20s, but some of us are old enough to remember them.

Instead of a round table, we sit around a long rectangular table. And instead of Dorothy Parker, Robert Benchley and George S. Kaufman, you will soon meet the dozen of us who get together every other week to talk and write.

Our advice to you is simple. Write what you know. Observe, and see how others write. Keep at it. When you're stuck, take a break. You may be surprised at the memories you recall, the people who show up, the truths you discover. Put your work out before this group of intelligent, interested listeners. They will help you to refine your own ideas and craft, and you will be well entertained by the stories we all share. Use writing to introduce yourself to all that you are: an unknown enemy – or an old friend – may linger within. And even if no one else ever hears your words, they are yours and you will have them forever – as will your children and your children's children. Enjoy the pleasure of creation. Playfulness is good; serious thinking is good, too. The combination is spectacular.

Our sessions are held in the seventh floor meeting room, where you can wander out onto the sunny terrace, or perhaps catch a whiff of alcohol from the weekly cocktail hour held here every Saturday afternoon. That's also one of the pleasures of North Oaks. Try it; you don't have to drive home.

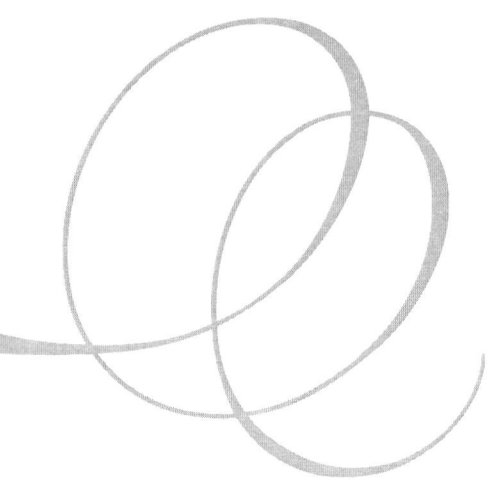

Spend the Afternoon

Avail yourself of every opportunity to enjoy, to learn, to create, to transform, to try to better understand the world and the people around you. Expose yourself to new experiences, new places, new music and art and reading. Remember that though life is now longer than ever before, it is still short to each of us. So do now whatever you still can, while you can. Spend the afternoon.

- MARGIE WARRES

Arrival

Outside My Window

It is three, perhaps four o'clock in the morning. I am a poor sleeper – wish it were otherwise. And I often find myself in the middle of the night in my easy chair, relaxing, watching TV or just pondering the state of the world – or, at the very least, the state of my world. I must fill in the long, lonesome dark hours of the night. Then, after, if the day is not to be rainy or otherwise overcast, perhaps I'll be treated to a thrilling, beautiful sight. Outside my window I can see the sunrise – a brilliant infusion of gold, orange and red slowly rising over the horizon. It is a sight to behold – dark, slowly evolving into light – the dawn of a new day. Darkness once again overcome by light! I smile to myself. The world is surely a better place by light. No matter how often I see it, awakening dawn is an awe-inspiring sight.

- BEVERLY SHARE

A Change

The time had come for me to say
had I decided yea or nay?

I had a nice home, the American dream
'til fate intervened to alter the scheme:
Medical problems had plagued my wife
'til sadly, they then claimed her life.
I learned the challenges of living sans spouse
without a partner who could manage the house.
Home repairs were sorely needed,
the damage severe, if left unheeded.
Single life turned out to be dull and dreary,
a condition of which I became quite weary.
My children suggested a retirement home:
"Join your contemporaries! Stop living alone!"
My independence reduced from one hundred percent?
What should I do: assent or dissent?

Lifestyle and finances, I reviewed again and again.
Should I accede to my children's campaign?
Back and forth my decisions went.
The patience of my children was nearly spent.
The last step of negotiations finally came.
Was I ready to sign my name?

The resident agent needed my check.
I thought to myself, "There goes your neck!"

With mixed views, I picked up the pen....
My address is North Oaks. I'm home. Amen.

• JOSHUA ROSEMAN

Letting Go

The Car

Though I felt underestimated and underappreciated, I also felt an understanding of my children's concern for their father's safety and well-being, as well as my own. I recognized that I was on the losing side of the argument for my continuing to keep and drive our Toyota Camry, which I loved. Everyone aware of the situation sided with my family except my husband Len who remained silent and understanding of both points of view. He had given up driving earlier because of deteriorating vision but he still had me to get him places, so there was no major calamity until now; and he supported my renewing my driver's license, which I did against the wishes of one of my sons. But I finally resolved to give up driving by selling my car myself (not to Carmax) to a nice, deserving person at a real bargain price, but for more than my children would have accepted. I guess I still maintained a modicum of control in a losing situation. But I couldn't argue with my son's contention that one never expected to have an accident, and they did not want to wait for one to happen.

The Pocketbook

When we decided to move to North Oaks, everyone told us to discard half of what we owned – clothing, furnishings, supplies, what-have-you – and most of our books, momentos, and albums. One of our friends, knowing how hard this would be to do, set up an urgent appointment to get me started with her experienced help at "tossing" – dresses, purses, suits. Further, she announced that she would be driving me, with all the chosen discards, to two places at the end of our designated day: Hadassah's "Scene II," and the Goodwill store on Fallstaff Road.

We did this to avoid my changing my mind, obviously. But in retrospect it was not the greatest idea, for I still nurture some regrets about what I could have retained. There were moments and longer intervals when I sorely missed some discards hastily dispensed with, which I could have managed to take along. I particularly recall a fine old leather pocketbook which I still miss – like a good old friend.

The Oyster Plates

The first thing I notice when I enter my apartment at North Oaks is my set of six hand-painted antique oyster plates. They were once a set of twelve, given to me by my father, who knew his antiques well. When we moved to North Oaks, I did not plan to give any of them up. However, every antique dealer who came to buy anything from me wanted them. I resisted until one clever dealer offered an extravagant price and suggested that perhaps I didn't need them all, which tempted me and I sold a number, leaving myself with six.

I wondered if I would regret this reduction, but it seemed sensible under the circumstances. I have held onto a few family antiques, such as a glass punch bowl we've used for holidays and whatever festivities came up through the seventy-two years of my marriage. Who will want it next remains to be seen, but I hope they will enjoy it equally as much and preserve it, though nothing lasts forever. Other serving platters from Greece and North Africa are lovely and useful for entertaining, but rarely used now. Smaller antique oyster plates I still relish, even for my lone use, whenever I can procure the raw cocktails.

Indeed, six is a sufficient number for an attractive display and also for serving on the rare occasions that I can get fresh oysters from Rhode Island or our own Eastern Shore. I am quite satisfied with my decision at this stage of my life, when I do not need more. The multi-colored pastel and gold plates add elegance and wonderful memories, transforming a small gathering into a festive special occasion.

- MARGIE WARRES

Retirement Uncorked

If you want to be entirely free
retirement, it's said, is the place to be.

As time goes by and you're finally there
here are some thoughts I'm willing to share:

After the grueling world of work
a plan for retirement must be uncorked.

Plan to have friends to share this stage,
companionship to ease the moody days.

Keep family and friends part of your group.
Good vibes will emerge with the family troop.

An exercise regimen, as much as you can do
will certainly serve to benefit you.

Eat to enjoy, yet keep it nutritious.
(You can find the "fit" menu if you are ambitious.)

The mind, too, must stay in shape
to prevent your memory from making escape.

When no other duties are scheduled for you
will you not yearn for a challenge or two?

If you haven't engaged in the arts in the past
discover your talents, explore at long last.

Nurture mind, body and spirit, a prescription for all.
Then, nothing can stop you from having a ball.

- JOSHUA ROSEMAN

Decoding North Oaks

The dining room is on the second floor and the café on the first. Treadmills on the eighth and Senior Aerobics on the second, but Chair Yoga on the first with the pool table next door. Coming from the elevator, the library is on the left and my mahjong game on the right.

So much to remember. Wait a minute, I'm supposed to be somewhere at 2:00, I think. What is it? Better check the weekly calendar. Oh, Music class, in Wilson Hall. What floor is that again? Should I ask the front desk? Maybe I'll call Edith. She's been here a long time and is always happy to help.

Who was that who invited me to dinner tonight? I think it was that nice couple, Lois and Sid. Or was that tomorrow night? So many invitations, so many new names! Shirley tonight, but which one? There must be ten Shirleys at North Oaks. Also two Goldies and three Estelles. Four Rosemans (not all siblings), and two sisters who have different last names. Two Blooms and a Blum, a Scherr, a Share and a Sherr, and then that ultimate tongue twister Wartzman, and Waxman. I'll just go down to the Oak Room and see who calls me over.

Lots to learn and remember. That's good; keeps your mind sharp. Gotta go now. The Foreign Policy Association is doing a program on Great Decisions and after that, physical therapy. What floor is that?

- MARTY WAXMAN

A Peek

Philip Lopate's essay "A Portrait of My Body" details his commanding stare, ironic smile, long, lanky legs and quirky cuteness.

What can I tell you about myself? My stare is blank much of the time and squinting the rest; at 5'6" my legs are surely not long and, at 86, my cuteness is appreciated only by our two-and-a-half-year old great-granddaughter Kaitlyn. So what is there of interest? Hair!

No, I don't have what Lopate might call a head of burnished ringlets that make a golden aura. But around the age of 15 a beard began to make an appearance on my boyish cheeks, and I was shaving soon after. I also noticed that my eyebrows became thicker, like those of many of my mother's family. My hair needed trimming at the barbershop more often than most – a mark of maturity. As I got older, I found that after shaving in the morning, I could feel the stubble in the afternoon – not Five O'Clock Shadow, but Two-Thirty Shadow. If we went to services at 10 a.m. and the symphony at 8 p.m., I would need a second shave.

Meanwhile, though, my hair began to thin at the crown, and one of my young daughters observed that if it continued, she would give me back to my mother. That was disconcerting. I so feared the reflection when the barber held up a mirror that over 30 years ago I stopped going to the barber altogether and now trim my hair myself.

I'm not a member of an Orthodox congregation, and do not wish to act falsely. But I do wonder whether the time has come to follow the Biblical commandment to cover one's head and begin to wear a yarmulke at all times.

• MIKE ROSEMAN

A Pest

As a new resident at North Oaks, I had many adjustments to make. My priority was settling into my apartment. I had always lived in my own house, so moving into such a large building of people was new to me. I wanted to make the apartment cozy and attractive, to reflect what is important to me. It is my retreat for peace and quiet.

One evening I was sitting in my living room reading a book, when I looked up and saw a black creature crawling around my bedroom. It saw me and flew under my bed; I jumped up, grabbed my keys, and flew out into the hall. I was shaking as I ran to my neighbor's and rang the doorbell. I used her phone to call the front desk, and they sent a security guard to investigate. He said the mouse was gone, and I told him, dramatically, *I am not sleeping with a mouse under my bed.* He assured me that a mouse would not hurt me; that they would send someone the next day and set mousetraps. I imagined the sound of the traps and the mice squealing and dying. Yikes!

How did I survive the night? I piled up my bed with my bed skirt, pillows, and comforter. I pulled them around me and made a barrier to protect me and prayed. Somehow, I endured. So, as it turned out, did the mouse.

Two weeks later I had another mouse visit, the same routine: more mousetraps, no caught mice. The exterminator came in but could not explain how they were exiting the apartment. Then all was peaceful for a time and I relaxed my watch. Recently, though, I saw another mouse creeping.

I know North Oaks allows pets to live with residents, providing comfort and companionship. But North Oaks, I am too old now. I am not looking for a pet!

- LEE RUBIN

Every Evening and Once a Week

Here's a riddle for you to solve:
What makes the North Oaks world revolve?

What happens each evening at North Oaks
plus once a week for resident folks?
It happens when we visit the doc
or lose our balance and take a flop,
hang a photo, need an emcee
or the picture goes black on our new teevee.
Ask to have our car brought 'round
or reclaim an item in the lost and found?
Mention our curiosities, share our yearning
for art or music or a bit of learning?
See a show or an Oriole game,
a film or a class? It's all the same . . .

With poise they prepare and serve our meals
and surely merit *Good Housekeeping* seals.
Whatever breaks, they're glad to repair
and when we need a ride, they take us there.
They schedule a slate of activities
that keep us busy as bumble bees.
So let's remember every evening and each week
and all those occasions both happy and bleak
to thank the skilled and caring team
that makes our North Oaks lives a dream.

- MARTY WAXMAN

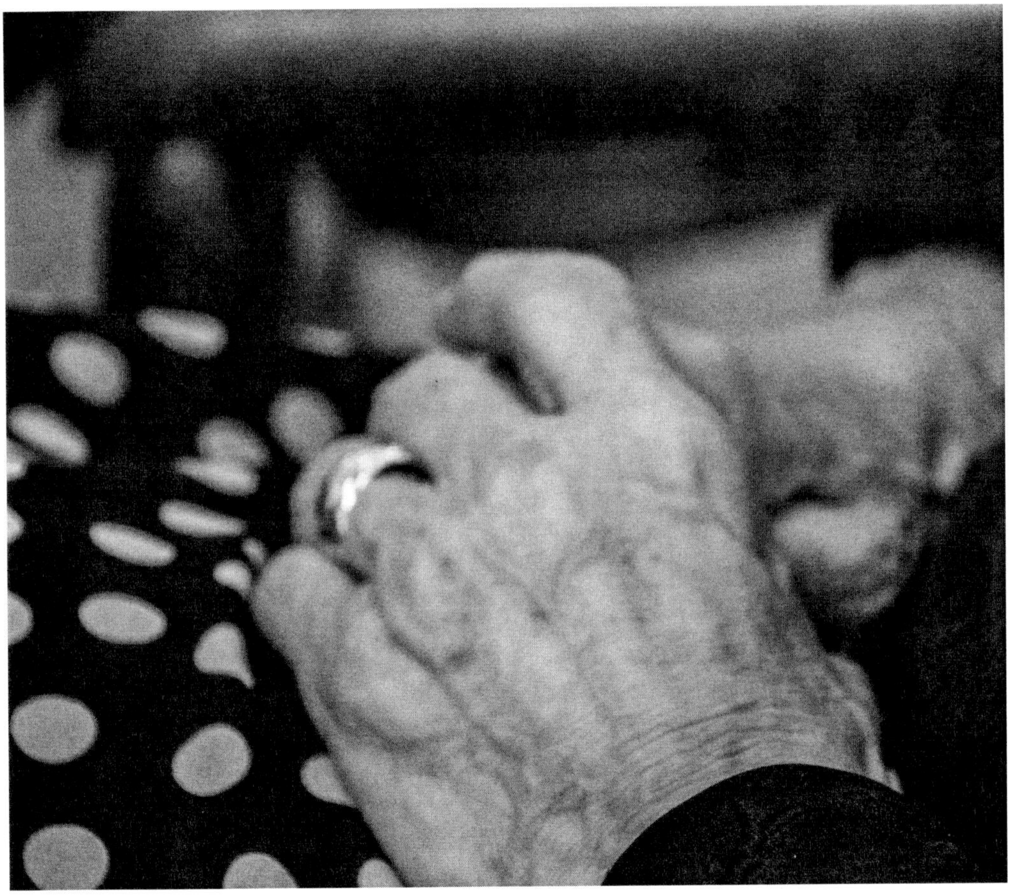

The Wye Oak

Now, when I look out the window of my North Oaks home,
I see the green of oak forests and think of her.

It was the time of *The Great Comet*
when Christopher Columbus was born.
Unknown to him was the land
on the shores of the Chesapeake Bay
where all kinds of trees grew.
In storms, many bent and broke.
But there was one tree – an oak – that held its ground
and became the Queen of the Trees.

Her Majesty grew taller each year.
Her tresses – those green leafy branches – swayed in the breeze.
Birds sang there, made nests, and laid their eggs.
Squirrels, those little misers, stockpiled the treasure of her many acorns.
In autumn, her leaves turned bronze and fell to the ground
awaiting the snow and her long winter rest.

Time passed, and she towered over everything in sight.
The Indians knew her
and later, the English settlers,
who named her place *Maryland*.
In modern times she, too, was named
The Wye Oak after *The Wye River*,
and visitors came from all over to revere her wonder.

And then . . . in the year two thousand and two,
a storm struck her down.
She cried out in agony as her trunk cracked and she fell to the earth.

The Wye Oak was ninety-six feet tall,
thirty-one feet in circumference;
her crown spread one hundred and nineteen feet.

She was five hundred and twenty years old.

• HILDA PERL GOODWIN

Innocence

The First Kiss

Adam and Eve dance to the music of the snake,
its hiss a seductive whisper on the wind;
the wind that dries the sweat upon their bodies
and leaves their mouths as dry as snake pits.

The apple Eve accepted from the snake
was polished and offered by Eve to Adam
with downcast eyes and blushing cheeks.

Its juices filled their mouths with pleasure
and they first pressed their lips together
to share its shivery delight.

- CAROL SUPLICKI

A Good Choice

Little did I realize that sunny May day as I skipped home for lunch that my life was to change forever.

Was it only four months earlier that my dear father David had gathered my brother and me upon his lap and said, "How would you like to have a new mother?" My brother who was ten and remembered his beautiful mother Ida so well immediately said "no," while I, who was seven, said "yes."

Mrs. Eberg, our housekeeper, opened the door as she always did in response to my ring, and she seemed very upset. "She's here," she whispered, and her eyes blinked rapidly as they did when things didn't go as she wanted.

I raced into the kitchen and there she stood at the stove cooking scrambled eggs.

"Miss Newman," I said. "It's great to see you again. Morton and I had fun at your house over the Christmas vacation."

Miss Newman turned off the gas, whirled around, hugged and kissed me. "I'm not Miss Newman anymore," she laughed. "I'm your new mother."

So began a love affair between my new mother and me that lasted for 17 years until the day she died in my arms. I never called her my stepmother; heaven forbid! She was always my "second mother," but as the loving person she was, I only called her "Mother Dear."

Why did I love her so much? Finally I had a mother like all my friends did, and what a special one at that. She thought I was the nicest girl she knew, and the smartest. I was the best mannered too; Emily Post was very important in her life and consequently in mine, adhered to almost as closely as the Bible.

I am sure my mother Ida, who died when I was barely five, must have said in heaven, "David dear, you made a good choice."

• LORRAINE GELULA

Vice President Nixon

I recall Vice President Nixon steering his simple blue car into our driveway in Rehoboth Beach, Delaware, with his wife Pat beside him, and two young daughters in the back seat. He was not escorted by aides of any kind, on a family trip arranged for him by a political friend who knew my father.

Ours was a large house. They stayed in the other apartment for at least a week or two. Pat went around with her hair in pin-curls much of the time, and Vice President Nixon often took our older son Steve sightseeing with his girls. One time they went to a nearby beach where an old ship had been sunk and later partially salvaged. It was called something like "Million Dollar Beach." This was the only time to my knowledge that children came back with actual old coins from that wreck.

One night, Steve was invited to sit at Nixon's right at a long dinner table on the front porch. He was about 12 years old then, sitting at the hand of the vice president.

The lack of ceremony and protection was quite remarkable even at the time, although Rehoboth has remained somewhat untouched in that sense. The house was at 29 Virginia Avenue in the town proper, on the lake surrounded by geese in the back and with the ocean and boardwalk visible from the front. If you drive by it today, you might see a young couple reading on the front porch, and children riding their bikes, unmonitored and carefree on the quiet street.

- MARGIE WARRES

The Bayonet

One object has been on my mind for almost 69 years – a U.S. army bayonet. In the summer of 1944 the draft called me and I was sent to an infantry basic training camp in Georgia. The courses included instruction in the use of this big knife attached to our M-1 rifles. It was attached by a slot on top of the grip, which fit onto a lug on the underside of the rifle, and a circular hilt, which fit over the muzzle.

One day we spent hours stabbing, slashing and slitting straw-filled dummies representing the Axis foes. Then we were directed to an area of trees and bushes and hilly areas for "close combat practice." With bayonets fixed, we spread out and advanced with care, the rifles loaded with eight round .30 caliber clips. The idea was that certain enemy soldiers depicted by cardboard dummies would suddenly appear from behind a tree or bush or hill and we were to aim and fire our M-1's. So when a "Japanese soldier" popped up several yards away, I immediately aimed at it and fired. The usual blast had a certain metallic tone to it and as I lowered the rifle I saw that the bayonet was no longer attached to it, and in fact was in the grass several feet in front of me! When I picked it up I saw that the circular hilt was no longer a circle but two twisted half circles, apparently torn apart by my bullet. This stunned me. I put the bayonet back in its scabbard on my belt and returned to the barracks without doing anything about it, still puzzling it over and over. (When in doubt, do nothing, I thought.)

A few weeks later the captain had us lined up for inspection and when he saw the hilt peeling out of the bayonet scabbard, his eyes popped; he pulled the bayonet out, glared at it and finally asked me, "What the hell happened here?" While I told him he kept shaking his head and sent me to the supply sergeant for a new one. I was charged about $6.99 from my month's pay for the replacement. After that, the captain shook his head whenever he saw me. I was told I was fortunate that the muzzle of the rifle didn't shatter into fragments because of the closeness of the hilt, and injure my face and head.

I didn't even hit the Japanese target, the remains of my bullet going who knows where.

- MIKE ROSEMAN

Playing War

I was seven years old in 1941. When did I hear about Pearl Harbor? When did I understand what it meant to our country and to our lives? My parents heard it on the radio that Sunday and I absorbed some of their distress and anger at the news.

From then on, war became a way of life. We saw newsreels at matinees. We collected rubber, metal, and tinfoil for the war effort. We had bombing raid drills. We played war.

• CAROL SUPLICKI

The First Time I Set a House on Fire

The first time I set a house on fire was in March, 1939, just prior to my 13th birthday and my Bar Mitzvah. We lived then on Chatham Road in the Forest Park area, not far from Liberty Heights Avenue and Garrison Boulevard. With Mel Bender, a friend my age, we built model aircraft; some flew, some didn't, and none lasted too long. One afternoon, my dad was in his office in the Canton area, Mom was downtown shopping on Howard Street, and my five-year-old sister was out somewhere with the part-time maid. Mel and I decided to retire a banged-up biplane model by recreating scenes from Errol Flynn's *Dawn Patrol* and launching it on its last mission, on fire. In the driveway next to the house, we lit it up and tossed it aloft. The plane burned briskly, being constructed of very flammable materials, and hit the driveway as ashes and embers. I took a garbage can out from under the back door porch and told Mel that we'd better clean up the driveway, and to make sure everything was put out. So we shoveled the remains into the can, put it back under the porch and strolled up to Liberty Heights Avenue to get some ice cream.

We ambled back about 30 minutes later. As we turned the corner at Chatham Road, we saw several fire department vehicles in the street in front of my house at 3705, and I thought, "We're dead!" Approaching, the lady caring for my sister Rita came up and breathlessly told me of coming home to see smoke at the back of the house. Mel and I, still licking ice cream cones, got closer and saw the scorching, but the fire had been put out. The firemen weren't sure what had happened, and of course it was a surprise to us, we'd been blocks away. Then Mom appeared, just walking up from the streetcar stop and almost collapsing when she saw the crowd. Once she saw Rita and me, and the maid and Mel, she calmed down somewhat, and we told her how we had come upon the scene. I had a definite feeling that Mom knew something was left out of my narrative, but she said nothing. Eventually, the insurance company paid for a new kitchen and porch, and my Bar Mitzvah the following week was not celebrated in our house as planned.

I remained friends with Mel, and over the years Mom would, on occasion, casually ask him what we were doing that March afternoon.

She always got the same answer – we were blocks away getting ice cream. But for 42 years, until she passed away in 1981, she suspected that we had been involved; she was a sharp lady.

Mel and I still discuss the incident 73 years later. After that day, while we often re-watched *Dawn Patrol* and other war movies, we never again tried to recreate WWI.

- MIKE ROSEMAN

A Memorable Day

It was a summer day in late July of 1940. My sister Lola was sitting on the front porch of our row house, reading a book, when she heard the light tapping of an automobile horn. She went to the front railing and saw a blue Plymouth sports car parked in front of our house.

The driver was someone she had recently met, Morris Perl. So she gave a welcoming wave and he came up on the porch and settled himself into one of our wicker chairs.

The sound of the piano could be heard coming from the living room. I was practicing the lyrical slow movement of a Beethoven sonata, and when Morris asked Lola who was playing the piano, she explained, "It's my sister, Hilda. She was going to enroll at the Peabody Conservatory, but she changed her mind and came to Goucher instead. She's one year behind me. But she can't stay away from the piano, and sometimes I think she is sorry about her decision."

Meanwhile, hearing Lola's voice and that of an unfamiliar male, I went to the screen door, where I could see them without being seen.

And there he was! With a face like a movie star!! My heart went *ping*. Then I kind of eased out onto the porch, introduced myself, and settled down on our glider, rocking back and forth and back and forth, noticing out of the corner of my eye the way Morris was looking me over.

Later we went inside to the foyer, a space between the parlor and dining room where our electronic phonograph was located, along with our collection of Big Band numbers. As Benny Goodman and Tommy Dorsey played, Lola and I took turns dancing with Morris, and when he danced with me, it was as though we had been dance partners always. Lola wasn't a bit jealous because she was going steady with a medical student then, while I was trying to get over a broken heart.

Time passed, and it was close to 6:30, so we invited Morris to stay for dinner. We knew that Celia always prepared enough food for an unexpected guest. Dad's arrival home from his downtown radio and home appliance store was announced, as usual, by his automobile banging on the tin doors of his garage in the alley behind our house, bending it out of shape.

As soon as we all sat down at the table, Mother rang her Stieff Silver dinner bell and Celia appeared with the best fried chicken ever, Maryland white corn on the cob, fresh tomatoes, plus an apple pie to rival the fried chicken.

Since Morris was a guest, Dad did not give the usual report on the day's activities to Mother, who was Dad's bookkeeper. Instead, the conversation turned to the news in the *Baltimore Sun* of the imminence of war with Germany and what President Roosevelt had to say in his recent radio Fireside Chat.

The afternoon with the dancing, Celia's cooking, plus the interesting dinner conversation added up to an "A plus." And so, Morris visited again and again and again and again.

We were married on June 22, 1941. And Morris drew his draft number on December 8, 1941, the day after the Japanese attack on Pearl Harbor.

• HILDA PERL GOODWIN

Graduation, June 1943

I still have my Forest Park High School yearbook for the class of 1943, which includes me, Editor Birdie Falk, (later Hack), and classmate Goldie Wolfson (later Scheinberg), now fellow residents of North Oaks. Graduation was held in June at the old Polytechnic Institute on North Avenue, with 284 in the class. Mayor Theodore McKeldin presided – a good man who later became Governor. The ceremony itself didn't make a lasting memory, but the times did.

At graduation time the U.S. and her allies were flexing their muscles. American and British forces had finally overcome the Axis armies in North Africa and were poised to land in Sicily and then Italy. In Asia, U.S. units were preparing to move north from the hard-won Solomons to other Japanese strongholds. The Russians were making major moves to retake territory then held by Germany, and the U.S. and the Royal Air Force were increasingly bombing German installations in preparation for the following spring's D-Day. I was 17 plus three months old, a bit younger than most of the fellows who were 18ish, the majority of whom were headed to the armed forces by enlistment or by draft board. That was the main question then: enlist now or wait for the draft. Following my dad's suggestion, I enrolled in Johns Hopkins University, and went into the army in the late summer of 1944.

I look back and recall Bob who crashed in a B-29 in the Pacific, and Ray who dropped out of school, became a navy medic and died on Iwo Jima. Many others like myself served stateside, but more were overseas and most returned to pick up their lives where they left off after high school.

Over the years several class reunions were held, up to the 60th in 2003, each smaller than the previous one. At the first one in 1993, I was delighted to meet George, who I had thought died in Europe. Thank God that was false! Still, when I turn the worn pages in my 69-year-old yearbook, I feel once again the mixture of joy and anxiety that the 284 felt that June in 1943.

- MIKE ROSEMAN

The Back Seat

A terrifying surprise developed after my baby brother's carriage overturned while I playfully pushed him around a room in our home in Delaware. Only eight months old, he was not yet able to talk, but he had a special light in the eyes when we communicated together. I loved to see his mischievous glint and big grin.

I didn't have much time to enjoy that smile. Soon after the fall, he developed spinal meningitis; the country doctor, who came quickly as I recall, immediately placed him naked in a cold tub of water. To this day, I can hear beautiful little Arnold's screams – and the doctor's insistence that this torture was necessary – until he suddenly fell silent, dead at nine months on his way to his first birthday on August 15, 1926.

Truth to tell, I have often wondered if that carriage accident was somehow responsible for what transpired, though I have always been assured of the contrary. I still feel guilty for that long drive to the Philadelphia funeral parlor, with our lovely baby lying swaddled between my parents on the front seat, and me alone in the back. What a ride. What a loss.

- MARGIE WARRES

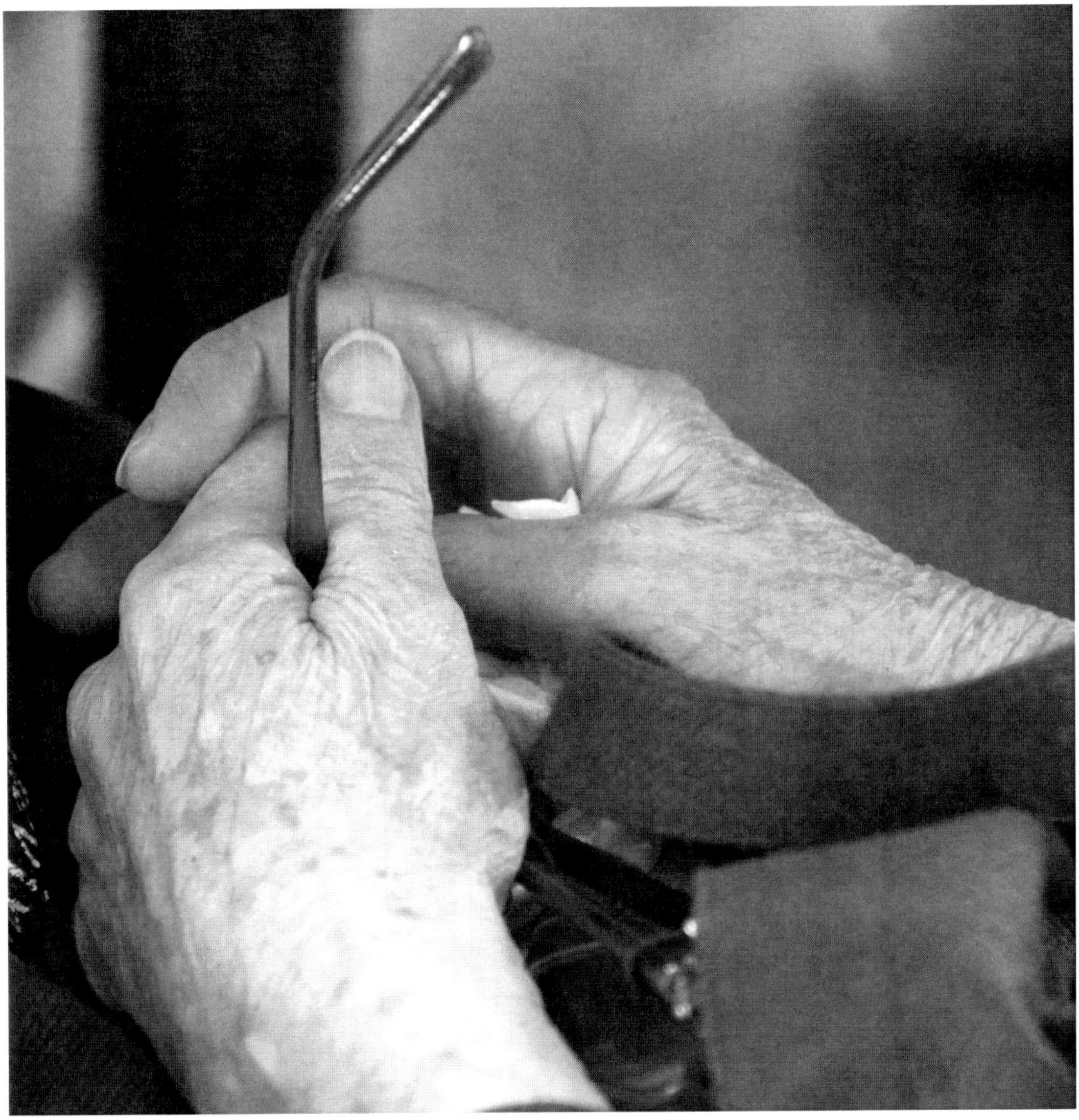

Ode to a Spider

Sweet little spider crawling up my wall,
surely you are not the fairest of them all
yet you do no harm to humankind;
I'll enjoy you, and pay you no mind.
Spin your lovely intricate web – I will watch.
Delicate, beautiful – no artist could match.
Spiders go about just plying their trade,
so my children – be not afraid!
It's been grand watching, my dear little friend,
but, alas, all good things must end.
I've feared you not, oh gentle spider of mine,
I wish you'll come back another time.
Would that all God's creatures were more like you,
quietly going about the jobs they do.
Perhaps all hatred and war would then cease
and the world live joyfully in loving peace.

- BEVERLY SHARE

Defiance

The Eight-Second Hero

The United Nations Military Force and the North Koreans had called for truce talks. I was a few months short of 24 years old when the 7th Division was replaced and we were sent into a valley away from the front lines and bivouacked there.

I was packing up when Captain Meadows saw me and said, "I was asked for a loan of a Communications man. Hurry up and finish packing and jump on that truck that's roaring its engine." I climbed aboard the truck with about two-dozen others. When we arrived at our destination, the sergeant in charge said, "Go to that camping area." I saw a 20-man tent where I assumed the entire group would be sleeping, so I went there to pick a good spot. I was wrong. I was the only one to sleep in that tent. We were ordered to meet in 30 minutes.

When the Sergeant saw me he asked who I was. "I'm your communications man," I said. He said, "I don't need a communications man, I need a cook. You're the cook." I didn't know how to cook. They gave me two Korean helpers. I remembered my mother frying things, so I emptied a #10 cooking oil can into a pot, and showed the Koreans how to cut the steaks and fry them. The men came off the line sweating and hungry. I served the steak along with potatoes and vegetables, and they loved it. I learned that the group was experienced in building fortifications, and the Korean unit of a dozen men was to be trained to build a new front line in the event the present line was breached.

The next day they told me they had chickens and I told them, "I don't know how to prepare chickens," so they called back to their unit and got a cook. I was free.

That day I saw a corporal heading up the hill to where the new front line was going to be built. I asked him if I could join, to see what was going on. He said, "Sure," and took me up a gulley where I saw nothing was done. It appeared that the unit pretended that they didn't understand English. I knew the officer did since I spoke to him the day before. In fact, he was an English teacher in a Korean high school before the war. I went back with the corporal and two Korean interpreters. Halfway back the corporal climbed a rock, making him over eight feet tall, turned to me and said, "Go into that village and get me two women." I said, "No way." He reached for the .45 in his belt, so I turned my M-1 rifle to him with my finger on the safety. He acted like he came from Colorado and was used to handguns. We eventually both moved our hands away from our guns, and then he repeated the order, thinking I was just a cook without front line experience. He repeated the order a second time and made a serious move toward his .45. I pulled my M-1 on him again, this time with the safety off, and his arm froze halfway between his shoulder and his belt; I had beaten him to the draw. I remembered the Jewish Chaplain telling us before we went overseas, "Jewish Law says if a man is trying to kill you, kill him first." Finally, the corporal took his hand away and ordered two Koreans to get him two women. I went on to the campsite.

A little while later I headed back and saw the corporal zipping up his fly. He said, "Your turn." I replied that I wasn't interested, and walked away. I turned and saw a mother staring at me with her 16-year-old daughter peeking from behind her. My thoughts went back to when I was 14 years old and someone showed me a newspaper account of when Poland was invaded in July 1942; it was a picture of a German soldier and a teenage Jewish girl, and the caption said he took her in the woods and came back alone. I felt like shooting the corporal for raping the women but realized I was the only Jew in the unit; I would be court-martialed as a Jew killing a Christian and be sent up for a long time. I had no witnesses. The Koreans wouldn't admit to anything; if they did the unit would kill them on the spot. I thought I should help the women, but who knew where they lived.

I went back to my tent, undressed, and slipped down to the spring and waterfall a few yards below the tent. I took my wallet, soap and a towel, and when I returned to my tent I noticed that my clothes were laid out. When I checked the pockets of my shirt, though, I found the grenade I carried was missing. In the other pocket was my Jewish Bible, which was not taken. I figured that the corporal had my grenade. I proceeded to dress, but someone must have been watching, because as I reached for my left boot, the long side of the 20-man tent was raised from both ends. I looked out and the two-dozen men were sitting on the bank. I see it's showtime. I'm back in high school handling the lights and doing bit parts in the theatre productions.

Then the corporal tossed my grenade just out of my reach; I had maybe eight seconds to get rid of it. First I thought maybe the powder must have been removed, like they did to the duds in basic; but if not, the other men were too close to the grenade and would also have been killed or wounded. Grabbing the grenade, I slipped on my boot, and yelled, "IF I DIE YOU WON'T SEE A JEW AS A COWARD!" I thought better of tossing it to the men in case it was a live grenade, so I did a V-turn to the canvas door and threw the grenade out. Then I sat down where I sat before, ignoring the men and focusing on tying my shoe. When I looked back up the canvas had been lowered.

I sat there, thinking, *this corporal threatened me three times. The next time he is liable to sneak up on me while asleep and kill me. Trust in the Almighty.* The canvas door opened up and it was the corporal saying, "That's the bravest thing I ever saw." He was scared. He repeated it.

I said, "Cut the crap, what happened never happened."

"Right," he said.

I said, "Let's try that again; nothing happened."

Again he said, "Right." I assumed his comments reflected the opinion of the other two-dozen men.

The next day we saw at least 200 Korean soldiers with digging tools heading to the new front. Evidently they had started to communicate. We were ordered to pack up, we climbed aboard the truck, and I was returned to my outfit.

• HOWARD J. COHEN

A Story I Don't Want to Tell

This is a story I'm reluctant to tell and often recall with considerable discomfort.

In May 1965, my wife was scheduled for her second surgery at Johns Hopkins Hospital after they discovered cancer the previous fall. I was filled with anxiety and fear and was trying to calm our two young daughters, my mother-in-law, and my mother. The day before surgery, Bunny gave me her wedding ring, inscribed with both our names, to keep until she was in recovery.

The morning of the surgery, I dropped off some clothes at the cleaners on the way down to the hospital. Later that day, after surgery, I was with my wife and she asked me if I'd put the ring in a safe place, and I was speechless; I had forgotten about it and couldn't recall putting it away. When I got home I searched all over – no ring. Recalling the cleaning, I called the owner the next day and thankfully, they had recovered the ring from a pocket and I could pick it up that afternoon. I visited Bunny that day, much relieved, and told her of my forgetfulness and redemption. She seemed better, and I was praying for a good report from the doctors.

At the cleaners on the way home there was one older man whom I didn't know at the counter. I told him my story and he claimed no knowledge of a ring, no one had told him anything, the boss was away, come back next week. I told him of Bunny's surgery and how important it was that I bring her the ring, at once. He replied that he knew nothing, couldn't leave the counter, come back next week.

At that point I felt something come over me that I had never experienced – a blind rage of anxiety and impatience and I shouted, "I'M COMING IN TO LOOK FOR THE RING AND DON'T TRY TO STOP ME!" He flinched, raised his hands and sputtered, "Don't hit me – I'll look, I'll look." Then he scooted around and in a few minutes found a small bag with my name on it on a desk. He gingerly handed it to me, I grabbed it and left without a word, got in the car and sat there, sweating and trembling like a leaf. God fobid, I could have killed him, I thought, and realized I was frightened. Eventually I got myself together and went home to the daughters, showed them the ring and acted calm. That night I remembered my childhood, when I dodged arguments, avoided the wild kids and never hit anyone with more than a friendly slap.

Some days later I picked up my cleaning. The man wasn't there, and I never saw him again. Thankfully my wife, wearing her wedding ring, was able to come home the next week.

Since then, I've been exasperated and angry, but never like that day in 1965 when blind rage was fed by fear and disgust at my carelessness with Bunny's wedding ring.

• MIKE ROSEMAN

History Lesson

After discharge from the army, I contacted my previous employer, Sylvania Electric Products. They informed me that my job had been filled, but by law they were required to give me an equivalent job. Since I was studying chemistry, they offered me a job in their Atomic Energy Division. I agreed to the transfer and reported to the facility in Bayside, Long Island. My new employer informed me that this was a new era; my previous army and navy clearances were insufficient and I now needed Atomic Energy Clearance.

When, five months later, I was finally summoned to the Manhattan Office of the AEC (Atomic Energy Commission), I was invited to a room with four men: two lawyers, one stenographer, and one man who repeated everything I said into the recorder. I assumed one lawyer was from the FBI and the second from the AEC. The questioning began.

"How often do you see your sister?" the first lawyer asked.

"What does my clearance have to do with my sister?"

"Answer our questions or leave without AEC Clearance."

I told them that before I went into the army I saw her as often as I could.

"Once a week? Twice a week?"

"Please stop recording and let's talk," I said. "What does this process have to do with my sister? I was just discharged from the army with the Presidential Unit Citation, Combat Infantry Badge and other battle field medals."

They explained. "In 1938 your sister signed a document from her union, the International Ladies' Garment Workers' Union."

"She is not a Communist," I said. "She is an Orthodox Jew! Plus, in 1938, I was ten years old! Are you holding up my clearance because of this?"

"No," they said. "In 1948, your father joined the American Labor Party."

"So what?" I said. "I would have done the same if I could have voted."

All four men stirred in their seats, thinking it was a confession.

"Don't you guys do your homework?" I snapped. "Keep the recorder on. In 1948, President Truman was running for president and he had promised the prime minister of England, Mr. Atlee, that he would abide by his request not to partition Palestine. Our congressman died and we had a special early election to replace the congressman in our Bronx district. The Saturday before the election my father attended Saturday services. The rabbi explained that the rabbis had met and agreed to announce to their congregants a plan to influence Truman's decision. The District normally voted 80% Democrat, 20% American Labor Party, and a handful of Republicans. The vote that Tuesday was reversed: 80% voted for the American Labor Party and 20% for the Democrats. President Truman got the message and voted for the partition of Palestine. Three months later at the regular election, the vote returned to 80% Democratic and 20% American Labor Party."

After that history lesson, I concluded, "I fought a war *against* Communism to protect the right of every American to use the ballot box to express their opinion peacefully."

I received my clearance one week later.

• HOWARD J. COHEN

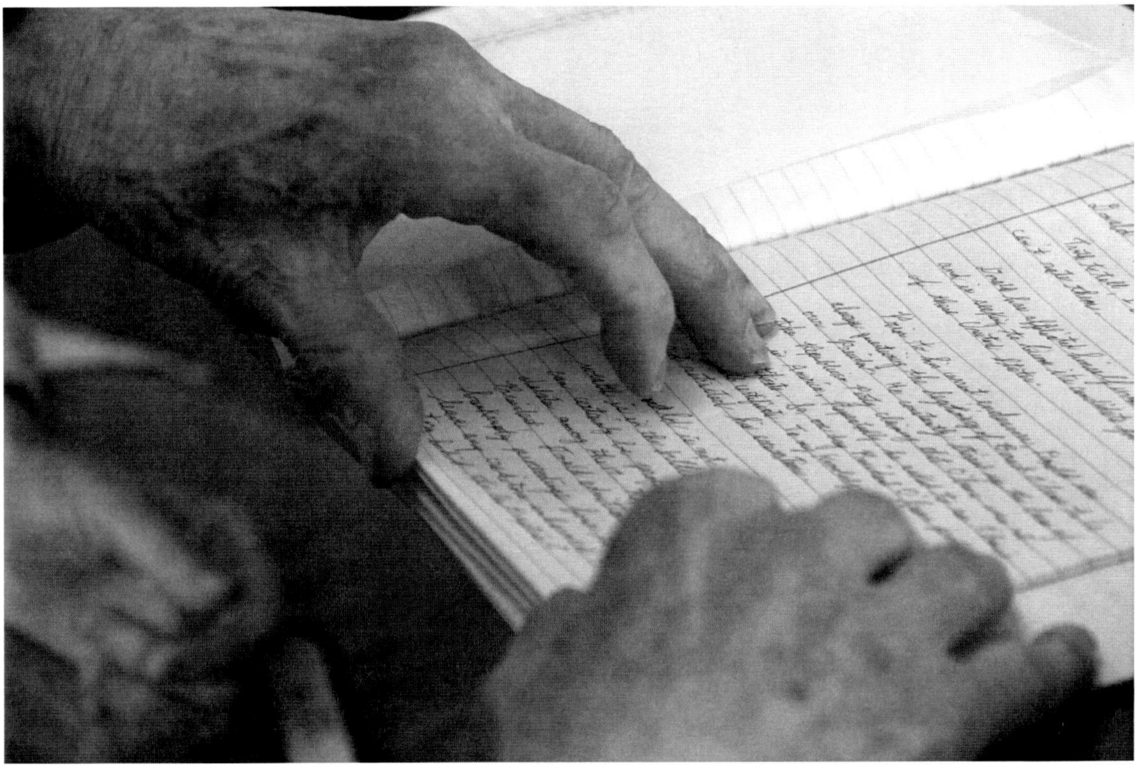

Glory

Miss Celeste B. Swenson was a Latin teacher par excellence. She loved Caesar and took a palpable delight in the violent retellings of his strategies and victories. She taught her first year high school Latin class well, and we learned.

But Miss Swenson did not like her students, especially not her few Jewish students. She was certain that all her students were cheaters. When she proctored one of her frequent vocabulary quizzes, she conscripted a boy to place her chair up on her desk, and climbed up. Like one of the ancient gods, she presided over the classroom, fiercely looking down on us.

Miss Swenson saw no reason to hide her attitudes toward the students; this was before the days of political correctness, and she could fathom no reason to be apologetic. She often said to a Jewish student who missed the correct translation of one of Caesar's battles, "You people do not appreciate the true glories of war." The day before Yom Kippur, she announced, "There will be a test tomorrow. It will be my great pleasure to give a zero to anyone who is absent."

To this day I remember – and detest – Celeste B. Swenson. But I did learn Latin, and continued to study it with pleasure for many more years, even as the boys who lifted the chair were drafted and I prepared to become a teacher. I remember the vocabulary and the declensions, but I still do not appreciate the "glories of war."

- EDITH SHERR

Report Card

The first time I went to school was in 1936 in Nottingham, England, not knowing any English. The principal, Miss Hancock, who was very nice, called me and two other girls into her office and told us that if she heard us speaking German together, we would be punished. She assigned an English-speaking girl in our class to each of us. The name of my appointed friend was Anne.

The first time I got a report card at Christmastime, there was a note at the bottom: Hilde talks too much.

Obviously, I had learned English!

• HILDE GUNDEL

I Don't Give a Fig

I have decided, at my advanced age, that there will be more and more things about which I do not give a fig. To begin, I've listed just a few:

1) The person with over 20 items in the 'Under 10' line at the Giant.
2) Sixteen-year-old waiters calling me "hon," or "honey."
3) People who talk incessantly.
4) Self-proclaimed authorities on every subject.
5) Doctors who keep me waiting an hour or more.

Life is just too short. We must all remember: don't fig the little. Save the fig for the big!

- BEVERLY SHARE

Trees

With apologies to Joyce Kilmer, Barbara Roswell and the group

I think I never want to see
another dirty, rotten tree.

A tree who in Autumn sheds,
making cars like unmade beds.

A tree who never lacks a reason
to give me work in every season.

A tree that, when growing old
develops roots oh so bold,

reaching down to pollute
and worse, next, to uproot

our lawn, that was once so fine.
I ask, Ain't that a crime?

- MARTY WAXMAN

Vengeance

At my age, my body betrays me all the time.

The dentist and I have lost the battle to preserve enough of my upper teeth to avoid a full denture. He and I will spend the summer preparing for the extraction of the last teeth and the transition to the replacement.

Every day, something in my hands aches. For a few weeks, the ache has been in my right thumb and forefinger. This is a familiar problem. All of the fingers and the thumb on the left hand have had shots for trigger finger, and the left middle finger was operated on. Another visit to the hand specialist is on the agenda.

One day, my feet and ankles swell. What the hell is this? A trip to the podiatrist, a trip to the vascular doctor, no blood clots, a prescription for compression stockings. Nobody likes compression stockings. I try them for a few hours. No dramatic change results. Maybe I'll be all right without them.

My skin doesn't fit any more. That thin layer of underlying fat that smoothed out the wrinkles in it has migrated to my midsection, which was better off without it. My skin also now develops bumps and swellings and discolorations, often in places where I can't even see them.

Perhaps this is payback for the times that I betrayed my body when I was young and careless of its long-term needs.

Maybe I forgot to brush my teeth. Sometimes I came home rather late and crashed without brushing. Maybe I did postpone the regular cleaning visits. Maybe it's genetic, or maybe dental care was not so good when I was a child.

Maybe my hands developed a repetitive motion problem. I did do a lot of typing, and later keyboarding, in my jobs. I even did a lot of writing with pen or pencil and paper. Maybe it's genetic, or maybe it's because I have small hands.

Maybe I ate too much and got too heavy for my feet. Maybe I didn't exercise enough. If I had been more popular, I would have done more dancing. Maybe it's genetic, or maybe it's because I have small feet.

Who knew I would live so long? If I had known, I might have taken better care of my body . . . or not.

• CAROL SUPLICKI

Doubt

I do not understand
why all babies are cute, yet there are
so many ugly adults.

I do not understand
why the need for so many new words —
twerk, mankini, hashtag, megapixels.
What do they mean? I assume
megapixels are many pixels — but what
is a pixel?

I do not understand these ~~four~~ things. I
do not understand.

Things I Do Not Understand

I do not understand
  Why it is so difficult to open the little cellophane packets of crackers.

I do not understand
  Why so many parts of my body are falling apart, while so many other parts of my body are fine. All of my parts are the same age.

I do not understand
  Why it is considered impolite to yell "keep quiet already" and walk away when someone is talking too much.

I do not understand
  Why all babies are cute, yet there are so many ugly adults.

I do not understand
  Why young people feel it necessary to announce every little detail on Facebook. Who really cares?

I do not understand
  Why the need for so many new words – twerk, mankini, hashtag, megapixels. What do they mean? I assume megapixels are many pixels – but what is a pixel?

I do not understand
  Why people do not grow taller as they age, instead of shorter. Then they would be able to look down on people instead of up at them.

I do not understand these things. I do not understand.

- BEVERLY SHARE

A Psalm over the Pacific

This I believe: that the Almighty watches over each and every one of us. Each night during my time in Korea, I said Psalm 23: "A Psalm of David" – I would not be surprised if infantrymen in other wars did the same thing – and though in Korea I was shot at by rifle, machine gun and mortar rounds, I left without a scratch. Two weeks before I was to rotate to the United States my father had a massive heart attack and I received emergency leave to return home. One belief-affirming experience occurred on that trip.

It was early in December 1951 when I left Korea. The army leased a four-engine civilian plane to fly military personnel to the U.S. We flew to Wake Island where we had breakfast, and then to Honolulu for dinner. Our next destination was California.

About two hours out, one engine on the right side caught fire and the pilot let it burn for what seemed like half an hour. The pilot eventually stopped the engine and extinguished the fire. We were then flying on three engines when, a short time later, the second engine on the right side caught. The pilot climbed higher in the sky and the oxygen masks dropped from the ceiling. We put the masks over our noses and mouths to breathe.

The stewardess came over to my aisle seat and spoke to the two of us: "In the event we hit the water I want you to pull the emergency exit door open and toss it into the water; then pull the cords on the two life rafts to start filling them with air and push them out the emergency exit while they're being filled."

I had her repeat the instruction. I looked down at the Pacific Ocean and thought, *I survived the war only to drown in the Pacific*. I said the "Psalm of David" and was surprised at how calm I was. The pilot shut off the burning engine and put out the fire. We were then flying with two engines on the left side.

Two Coast Guard planes showed up, one on each side of the plane, carrying large boats beneath them. We reached the Californian coast and proceeded to land, fire engines and ambulances racing alongside us on the runway. The pilot made a perfect landing while the fire department stood by, hoses aimed at our plane in anticipation of a crash landing.

The Lord is my Shepherd, I shall not want. He makes me lie down in green pastures. He leads me beside the still waters. He restores my soul; He guides me in straight paths for his name's sake. Yea though I walk through the valley of the shadow of death, I will fear no evil. For You are with me. Your rod and Your staff, they comfort me. You prepare a table before me in the presence of my enemies. You have anointed my head with oil; my cup runs over. Surely goodness and mercy shall follow me all the days of my life; and I shall dwell in the house of the Lord forever.

- HOWARD J. COHEN

Giving Up a Childhood Dream

Ever since I can remember, I had wanted to be a sports writer on a New York daily. In elementary school, I kept scrapbooks of newspaper clippings; I listened to baseball on the radio and went to Brooklyn Dodger double-headers and Madison Square Garden college basketball games and wrote stories. In high school, I was accepted to the journalism class and wangled a stringer's position with the *Brooklyn Eagle* reporting on high school games. At New York University, I landed a position on the *Washington Square Bulletin*'s sports staff.

In college, as in high school, I excelled in English, social studies and math, but was a dismal failure in French and geology. After my freshman year, tuition at NYU went up, if memory serves, from $13 per credit to $17. I was anxious to get out into the real world and used the tuition increase as an excuse to drop out.

I applied to all seven New York dailies plus the *Brooklyn Eagle* and the *Newark Star Ledger*, without success. Each told me that I would have to get started in the hinterlands, defined as every place outside of New York. I did land a part-time job at the weekly tabloid, *Sportsweek*, where the editor insisted I write under a pen name, Bat Masterson, Jr. I was the inquiring reporter, going to places like Grand Central Station and asking opinions on sports issues.

I continued to haunt the personnel offices of the dailies and, finally, bingo! An opening for a copy boy on the lobster shift of Hearst's *New York Journal-American*, 2 a.m. to 10 a.m. with a union-scale salary of 25 dollars a week plus 50 cents for night differential. After a few months in the noisy wire room tearing and sorting stories, I was assigned to the copy desk, seated around the rim-shaped table with three or four copy editors and the head copy editor inside the rim. They taught me style, ways to trim stories for available space, and the techniques of headline writing. My next move was to sit across the desk from the night editor, who gave me the responsibility to select the national and international stories for possible placement. I also worked with the photo editor, trimming photos and writing captions, and the makeup editor in the composing room, instructing printers on the placement of stories.

Then came a really great break: the college basketball scandals, charges that players on some of the country's top basketball colleges were being bribed by gamblers to shave points so they could beat the point spread. I knew some of these players from my neighborhood; I had played schoolyard basketball with them. I knew some of the suspected bribers, too, and even knew where the relationships got started – the hotels of the Borscht Belt where top high school and college players took jobs as bellhops and busboys and played on hotel teams. This impressed the sports editor, and I was assigned as one of the reporters to cover the story. I scooped the other papers on some of the aspects of the scandal and got a "battlefield promotion." I had made it; I was a sports reporter on a major New York daily. But we were at war with North Korea and just then my number came up and I was drafted.

After two years in the Army Signal Corps, I returned to my job as a sports reporter, but times had changed. Senator Joseph R. McCarthy of Wisconsin was capturing headlines and ruining lives by making unsubstantiated accusations such as "The State Department is infested with Communists . . . I have here in hand a list of 205 names . . . made known to the Secretary of State as being members of the Communist Party and who are still . . . shaping policy . . ." No names were ever revealed, but hundreds of other names were published in a periodical called *Red Channels,* which served as a blacklist, ending employment, breaking up families, and even leading to several suicides.

The *Journal-American* and some of its staff were part of the smear and blacklist apparatus. Every day brought false charges: "He is a red . . . She is a leader of a communist cell . . ." Careers wrecked, lives in ruin. I saw it happen, working in the same newsroom as some of the participants.

What was a young, liberal idealist doing among that gang of ghouls? After a few months, it was goodbye to the *Journal-American* and my sports writing career. Why did I give up my childhood dream job? In the words of Polonius: *To thine own self be true.*

- MARTY WAXMAN

My Obituary

I refuse to write my own obituary.
I trust my kids will be complimentary.

They'll say that I was wonderful in every way,
not the ordinary person you meet every day.

I was generous, kind, and cherished by all,
the perfect mother they love to recall.

Surely they'll mention my beauty, in and out,
the ideal of perfection – I have no doubt.

And all that I did for humankind,
my brains, my intellect, my facile mind.

All the world will know how perfect I was
but be careful – not too much fuss!

And so, my dear son, and my dear daughter,
include all the good things that you know you oughta.

I will not interfere in any way.
You must write it all down in your own personal way.

Unfortunately, I won't be around – so I'm pleading
write it all down so I can do some proofreading!

• BEVERLY SHARE

Wishing

Betty has a little sister. Irma has two little sisters. I am so jealous. When I complain to my mother, all she says is, "Keep wishing."

Every Friday dinner I split the chicken wishbone, and wish for a sister. Every night before bed, I look out the window for the first star and wish for sister. Then the day comes, and the baby arrives. A boy. I am disillusioned. And if that is not bad enough, when he is eight days old, there is a party for him in the hospital and I am not allowed to be there, but my younger cousin is taken to the party by my aunt. Who needs this brother? If he had been a sister, I am sure I would have been invited to the party and not sent to school. So much for wishing. I've lost faith.

A week later my mother and the baby come home. When I go over to look at him, one of my favorite aunts scolds, "Don't touch the baby!" What good was all the wishing? I was expecting . . . What was I expecting? A live doll to play with, I suppose. He cries all night long and I cannot sleep, so I fall asleep in school. I am mortified, and it is all the baby's fault. I will never wish again.

After a few months, he begins to smile, and always smiles when I come into his line of vision. I like that, but he is not my sister and I still feel cheated. Then he starts to babble, and whenever he sees me out comes Eely – his second word after Mama. I feel proud.

I begin to think this brother is okay. Not a sister, but definitely welcome. And I begin to wish again.

• EDITH SHERR

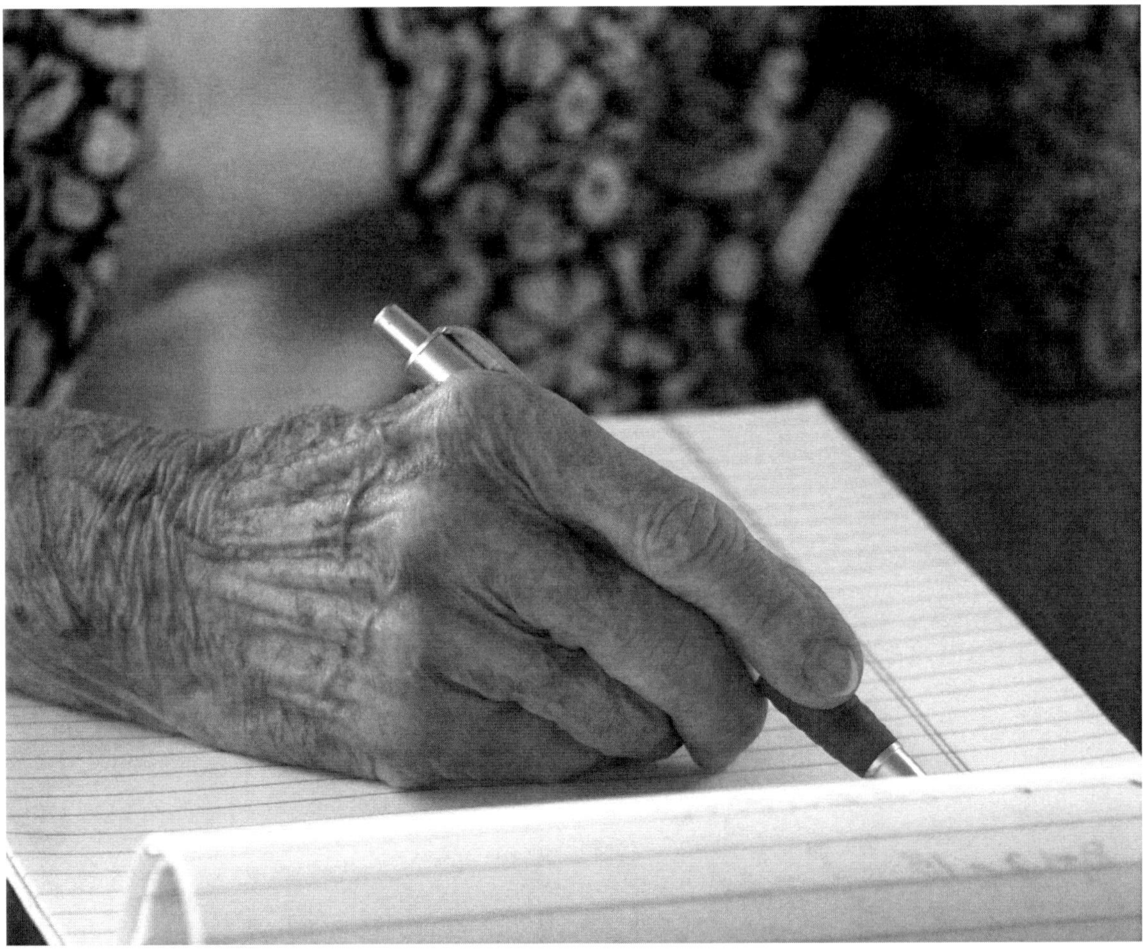

God and I

God and I have become much closer since we've been living in this tiny boat, and I know things about God now that no one else does. God experiences some of the same feelings I do, and gets moody at times when there isn't enough room or the seas are rough. God annoyingly always seems to get the last word, but I look up to him (her!) to guide us to a good harbor.

God and I have become like marbles in a box, rolling around, bumping into each other, sometimes skating along side by side. We make gentle clicking sounds; we bang into each other with loud clangs. Do we want to roll around together or be taken out of the box? Maybe God has the answer. I do not.

All of the gods and I have become like old friends. When I make wisecracks, they give me long sideways glances and refuse to comply. They don't lecture me anymore; they know I try to live a good life because I am a humanist. I respect my fellow humans, but abhor the inconsequential differences in belief systems and ritual that drive people apart, leading to hatred and war.

God and I have become like father and child. I look to him to copy his ways. He is gentle but firm, and I try to follow his path to live a useful, meaningful life.

God and I have become
Bosom buddies.
Our conversations keep me smiling.

God and I have become two ships sailing away from each other. I find myself shouting through a megaphone across the emptiness: Why do bad things happen to good people? When is enough ENOUGH?

God and I are acquaintances who have met again after being apart for many years. When I was a child, he was a friend of my parents. They knew him quite well, and therefore I did also. But as I grew up and my parents were no longer here, God left as well. In these later years of my life, God has come back into my life, as old friends are apt to do. He visits me often. The best friends are people we have known since childhood, and we understand and respect each other.

• THE WRITING GROUP

If

If I hadn't had those pesky little ants on my windowsill and *if* I hadn't placed the piano in my living room adjacent to the windowsill where the ants had been paying a visit and the exterminator was doing his job of getting rid of the ants and *if* the exterminator hadn't asked me *if* I played the piano and *if* I hadn't said yes I did and *if* he hadn't been Polish and had recently traced his lineage, *then* I wouldn't have become acquainted with a descendant of the great composer Chopin.

With the ants unwittingly awaiting their demise, I am moved to play the recording of the Third Movement of that Chopin piano sonata that is written in the style of a funeral march . . . *if* I only could find it in my collection of CDs.

• HILDA PERL GOODWIN

Release

Good to Be Out

I'm trying to be philosophical,
but it's no fun being in the hospital.
The food here is quite deplorable,
my entire stay not too enjoyable.
They do kindly give you a pill to sleep,
but in the middle of the night they do creep.
Vampires for blood – more and more
'til they get it all – a pint, two, three or four!
The nurses can't help it – it's their vocation,
still I wish for another location.
Don't listen to me – I'm full of hot air –
But lordy, lordy – it's good to be out of there!

- BEVERLY SHARE

Sixteen

I'm sixteen, supposed to be grown up and wise.
I'm in college, but I have closed eyes.
I'm scared. I don't know what it's all about.
I act brave, but I want out, out, out.

• EDITH SHERR

Home from Korea

I returned from Korea on a Red Cross emergency leave order after my father had a heart attack two weeks before my nine-month tour of duty was complete. In the army, if you served less than eight months in Korea, you would be sent back to Korea to complete your tour of duty.

I reported to Fort Dix, New Jersey, for reassignment in the States. They assigned me to Fort Totten in Bayside, Long Island, about an hour by bus and train from my parents' home in the Bronx. I reported to the Warrant Officer at Fort Totten whose anti-aircraft unit was meant to protect New York City from air attack – except they had no anti-aircraft on the base. The officer looked at my records and asked why I wasn't wearing my medals. I said I did not want to brag. He insisted I wear my medals proudly in the future and assigned me to a unit run by Lieutenant Rodgers.

Two days went by when I learned that married men got weekend passes if they were not assigned to duty. I asked if I could receive that privilege since I was on compassionate assignment. Permission was granted and I presented myself to my commanding officer and made my appeal. He ordered me to step into the next room where his two clerks were seated, both sergeants. He called the warrant officer and said, "Why did you send me a boy instead of a man?" I was burning. The two sergeants raised their voices to block my hearing. I turned around to them and yelled "Shut up." They shut up. To them, I was one of the first men back from an infantry company in Korea and therefore a killer. I listened to the rest of the lieutenant's belittlement until my commanding officer ordered me to report to the warrant officer at 9 a.m. on Monday. "Now return to your unit," they said. Later, I saw the Catholic chaplain and explained the situation, but he couldn't help.

I saw the warrant officer on Monday as ordered. He said, "Sit down," and started off by saying, "Who do you think you are?" He turned red-faced, telling me off. I just sat there looking at him; finally he said, "Why did you ask to see me?" I said I didn't, I was ordered here. He turned pale then and said, "What is this about?" I said, "Do you really want to know?" He said yes so I told him what happened, repeating the officer's jibe about sending a boy instead of a man. "You know I've earned my keep in this man's army," I said. He agreed. I said, "I want to be transferred out of this outfit. I earned the right to be called a man." He said, "Hold it. I will transfer you to another unit." I said, "As long as I get a pass once in awhile." He transferred me to a unit with two ROTC officers and an old southern army sergeant.

I had arranged to have my wedding on June 8th, but needed permission from my lieutenant for time off. I asked the sergeant for permission to see the lieutenant and he said he would ask for me. The clerk said that he told the lieutenant he saw no reason to give me a pass. We were bivouacking in Nutley, New Jersey, when he told me what happened and I asked permission to go back to Fort Totten, claiming I had a toothache. I went to the chaplain, who had just performed a marriage ceremony. I told him my problem and he said, "Ask for me if you have a problem. You will get your furlough."

After that I was given a ten-day furlough for my marriage and honeymoon. The unit was sent to the end of Long Island to fire anti-aircraft guns while I got a pass one week early and had only a three-day honeymoon. When I returned to the base I had five days left before being discharged on June 24, 1952. A different warrant officer called me in and asked if I wanted to re-enlist; I said, "You've got to be kidding." He said, "Say sir," so I said "Sir" and explained I was married two weeks prior, that I was drafted from CCNY with 90 credits, and that I would return to complete my degree.

Later I received a letter asking me to join the reserves. I tore the letter up. To quote Martin Luther King, "Free at last, Free at last, Free at last."

• HOWARD J. COHEN

No Heat

My classroom is cold. The whole school is cold. The furnace is broken, and the six-year-olds in my class are complaining. I have them sitting at their desks wearing their coats and even their hats. But what can I do? I can't warm them.

I give out drawing paper and ask for pictures of hot things. They get busy, and with their stiff little fingers they draw fires and beaches and suns and oatmeal and so many other hot things. The morning passes.

Miraculously, by noon, the heat is back on.

- EDITH SHERR

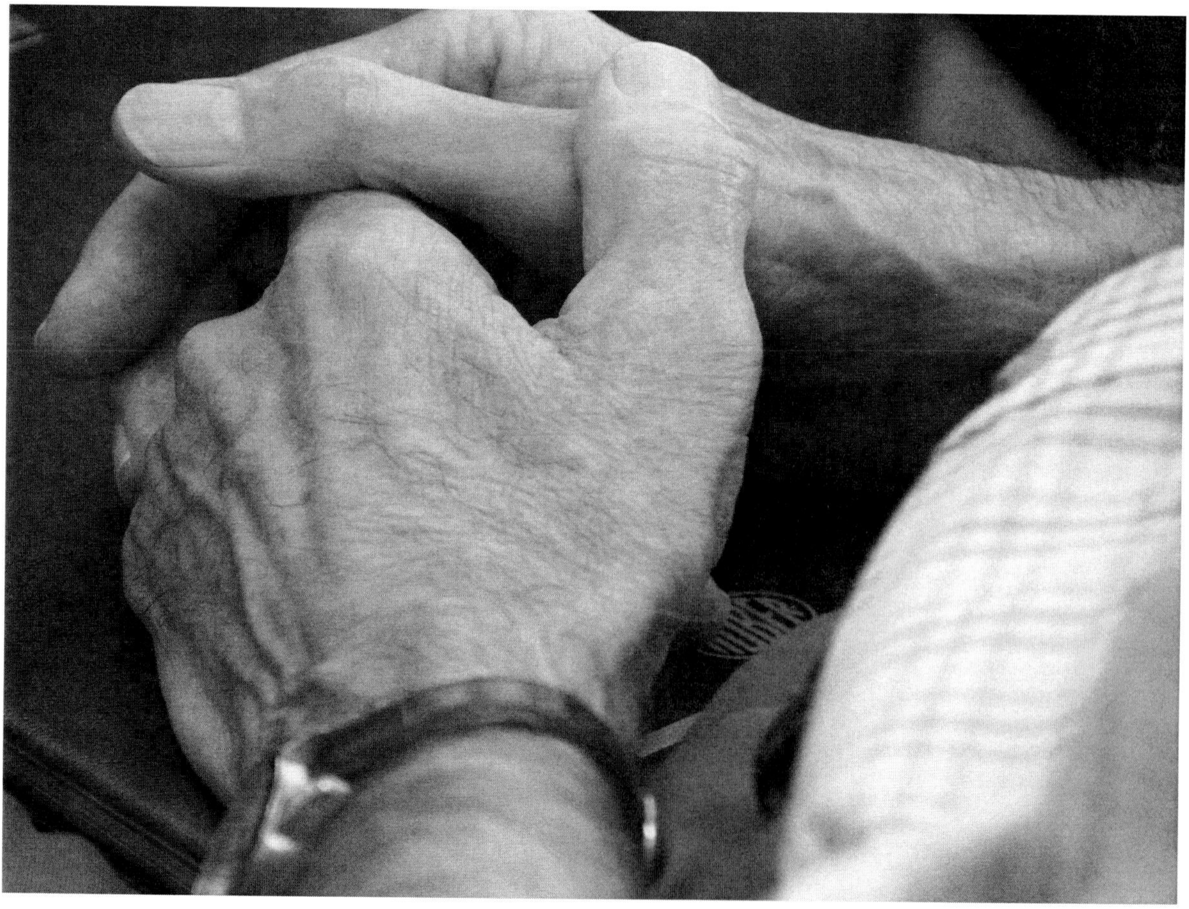

I Never Met

I never met Perry, and I never met Bing
but, oh, how I loved the songs they would sing.

Not like the drivel they sing today
I can't understand a word they say.

I could listen to Sinatra all day long
Steve and Edie and a touching love song.

I went on the Atchison, Topeka and Santa Fe
and left my heart in San Francisco by the bay;

danced by the light of the silvery moon,
and knew every last word would rhyme with June.

Alas, the lovely old songs of yesteryear
are gone forever, I sadly fear.

• BEVERLY SHARE

Uncle Louie and the Comic

My Uncle Louie was a table pad salesman eight months of the year and a personnel director during the summer season in my Zeida's small Borscht Belt hotel who always went for a cup of coffee to Field's drugstore in Loch Sheldrake when he had a problem as if they didn't have coffee at the hotel, which served three multi-course, multi-choice meals a day plus an open tea room in the afternoon and evening, and Uncle Louie did have a problem on Labor Day 1955 when the comic he had booked for the traditional midnight supper got sick and the booking agent called saying he had no replacement, so Uncle Louie called me over and said take a ride with me for a cup of coffee at Field's drug store and I did and as he was telling his problem to the counterman in this almost empty drug store, empty because everyone else was getting ready for the midnight supper about to happen at every Borscht Belt hotel, but there was one man sitting at the end of the long counter who overheard Uncle Louie and said, "You need a comic? I'm a comic," and Uncle Louie used his highly sophisticated interview technique and said, "Okay, make me laugh," and the comic did, so Uncle Louie offered him 20 bucks for the one night stand but the guy held out for 25 and Uncle Louie, pressed against the wall, gave in and the three of us rushed back to the hotel, Waxman's Overlook only a few minutes away and after the guests had their fill of corned beef, pastrami, potato salad, coleslaw, all strictly kosher, with plenty of cookies and rugelach, backed up by the four-piece band playing music of the big band era and, of course, klezmer, the comic gets up and knocks them dead, even Estelle and I are rolling in the aisle, but that's not the end of the story because now it's a few years later and Estelle and I are watching the Ed Sullivan show and it was a really big show where he introduces a new comedian who also knocks it out of the park and Estelle and I turn to each other and say, "That's the guy," and who do you think it was? Jackie Mason.

• MARTY WAXMAN

Every Meal a Banquet

For a brief period in the history of the New York Jewish community – perhaps a third of a century – the garment industry had a fifth season: the "slack season." No, not slacks; "slack" meaning a time of the year when the fashion market was slow. It happened every July, a time when the city was hot, a time before air conditioning, when the only places to get relief from the heat were "air cooled" movie theaters and Coney Island.

With union-negotiated two-weeks vacation, it was a time to go up to the mountains and that meant the Catskill mountains, popularly known as the Borscht Belt. Perhaps 500 resort hotels, almost all of them built, owned, and managed by untrained Jewish immigrants, were located in Sullivan and Ulster counties of New York about 60 miles from the city.

My grandfather, whom I called Zeida, was in the hotel business. This man who never learned a word of English somehow knew how to be a successful small businessman in his adopted country. First he ran a ma-and-pa grocery which he sold to buy a small hotel, the Capitol Mansion in Ferndale, New York, the heart of the legendary Catskill Mountain Borscht Belt. Three meals a day, each five, six, or seven courses, strictly kosher, a tea room open between lunch and dinner and then again after the social hall closed around 11 p.m., just in case you needed a nosh or a drink. The slogan was "Every meal a banquet," and it was true.

Entertainment and dancing to a four or five-piece band nightly. A full-time social staff, headed by a *tummler* (combination producer, director, emcee and comic) and including a girl singer and a second banana. Three nights a week there was a show, headlined by an act supplied by a booking agent – usually a comic or singer – and including songs and skits by the full-time staff. I still remember some names: Nat Keats, Stoogie Miles, Shirley Goldberg.... On weekends, Cantor Shimeleh Glatt came up to entertain the guests with Cantorial selections and Yiddish songs. When there was no show, it was game night, bingo, amateur night or a movie. Everything was included; nothing cost extra. All this for about $25 a week for a room with the bath on the floor or about $35 for a private bathroom. And they bargained!

Getting there was an experience. Few of the customers owned cars. Some came by railroad, air polluting steam engines with open windows choking the passengers. Some came by Short Line bus. And some came by *hack*. This was more expensive. The *hack* was a private limousine that seated seven passengers plus the driver and somehow (not very comfortably) held all their luggage, mostly tied to the top. Each passenger would be picked up at their home, some in Brooklyn, others in the Bronx or Lower East Side of Manhattan. It would take hours, but every seat would have to be filled to make it pay for the *hackies*. It would take a shoehorn to fit the seven passengers in, especially when two or three were obese. It took hours before it would leave the city. By then, there would be arguments about whether the windows should be open or shut, but when they got to Secaucus, New Jersey, all agreed shut to keep out the stink of the pig farms. By then, some kids would be gagging and yelling to stop the car – or even worse. As it approached the infamous Wurtsboro Hill, all held their breath and prayed the car with the heavy load would make it. Then, the famous sign of the Red Apple Rest, "Eat Here And Get Gas" would come in to view and all would heave a sigh of relief. After all, by then they were cramped into a tight space for six hours, and all needed relief in every sense of the word.

- MARTY WAXMAN

Breakfast in September, 1941

In 1941, I was living in England, but my parents were still in Germany. My sponsor had sent me to a boarding school to get out of the city, namely Nottingham. I had not heard from my parents in the two years since the war had started in Europe.

One morning at breakfast in September 1941, the principal, Mrs. Melbourn, came to the dining room and announced that she had to make an exception, and motioned me to come to her office. The mail was usually given out at lunchtime. Lo and behold, she handed me a letter from my parents. They had managed to get out of Germany and had flown to Spain, to wait for a boat to bring them to the U.S.

- HILDE GUNDEL

Legacy

Before North Oaks

A century before there was a North Oaks Retirement Community, our tall building on Mount Wilson Lane was a tuberculosis hospital. In 1913, my maternal grandfather was sent here from Baltimore City, where TB was of epidemic proportions, as it was in most large cities worldwide.

Wealthy Baltimoreans went to the Rockies, or the Poconos, or the Adirondacks for the standard treatment of rest and fresh air. Poor people came to the state sanitariums in Catonsville or Sykesville, or here to Mount Wilson, the highest point in Baltimore County.

TB had struck my entire family. My mother, who was five years old, and her sister, who was eight, were able to fight off the disease. Their baby brother, George, age one, and Uncle Leroy, 26, were not. Ultimately, my grandfather, too, was sent home to die.

My mother remembered the pennies placed over her father's eyes, I suppose to pay his fee to cross the River Styx. She remembered riding in a carriage to Baltimore Cemetery, where her father and brother George were buried. Her father was 28 years old.

The TB sanitarium was still operating in the 1940s, when my cousin, a visiting nurse, recalls coming up the mountain to see patients here. In 1946, streptomycin was found as a cure for TB, and the disease almost disappeared in this country. Though the Mount Wilson TB hospital closed many years ago, TB is more than a memory, and we're told that the recent resurgence of antibiotic-resistant strains keeps the current North Oaks staff vigilant.

- CAROL SUPLICKI

Evening Meal

Daddy's favorite things were his tools. He had a tool box with various kinds and sizes of screw drivers, hammers, pliers, wrenches, rulers, a level, a plane, and other items for carpentry and general work. He stored his larger, dangerous tools, like dragon-toothed saws, on the rafters in the basement, away from any child's curious fingers. On the occasions when Mother got him to go to Sears with her, he would disappear into the tool department while she was buying clothing and household items.

He always carried a penknife in his pocket, and he could cut a length of string or peel an orange for you. But his hands were his best tools. When my younger sister came home from the hospital weighing just five pounds, he formed a cradle for her in those hands. He could figure out how to refashion coat hangers into stands to hold a doll collection or he could raise a toast with a teacup at a party for those dolls. His hands were dexterous in spite of a childhood injury that left his right index finger webbed. He had cut that finger on a broken bottle. No doctor was consulted, and the home care didn't include splinting to keep the finger straight.

My hands were not so adept, but I proudly presented my parents with a small corner shelf made in junior high shop class. They were duly impressed. Years later, my mother told me that my father had reinforced it so that objects wouldn't slide off. When I started working with computers in the 1960s, they were known as "big iron," and I wished that I could share a laugh with my father over my unexpected career choice.

Our 1930s house had sparse closet space, so Daddy built cupboards in the small kitchen and bookcases in the living room. One evening, after Mother and he had a discussion about the advantages of an open floor plan, he went to the cellar and reappeared with a sledge hammer. He tore down the wall between the living and dining room, and repairs were done in a few days.

At his job for the American Can Company as a machinist first class, Daddy was a user and a maker of tools. He maintained the turbines and conveyor belts used in the manufacture of cans and other metal containers. He designed and fashioned whatever parts were needed to keep the lines running. He also used scraps of metal to create cookie sheets for us and a tool to pry ice cubes out of trays before manufacturers developed trays with built-in levers.

Daddy didn't wear any jewelry. When he worked around machines with moving parts, he didn't want to risk any metallic entanglements. He never had a wedding ring; marriages in the Depression were minimal by necessity, but my mother had a nice band with diamond chips. In the winter, he wore a fedora, never a cap, and a short leather jacket. He wore a leather belt and, when we acted up at bedtime, he would take it off, fold it in half, and snap it with a loud noise that sent us scurrying to bed. Years later my sister said that he beat us with his belt, but he never did – the snaps were frightening enough. I reminded her that Dad's father, who shaved with a straight razor, had beaten his sons with his razor strop. I remember touching it, a piece of hard leather about three inches wide and 18 inches long. Mother could deliver a spanking, but Daddy never did.

My parents enjoyed having friends over on weekends, and parties in the basement featured different themes as the seasons changed. In the winter, Mother would buy a peck of oysters from a huckster who drove his horse and wagon down our street. I think it was a pitch-in party, where the group that gathered shared the cost. My father had an oyster knife and did the shucking for the crowd. The summer would feature steamed crabs and Daddy could be counted on to share his crabs with a hungry daughter. There was often music, as both my mother and aunt were accordion players. They had bought their husbands harmonicas, although neither of the men had shown any talent for music. In fact, Mother swore that Daddy had a tin ear. They enjoyed popular music, and my father liked to tease us with the words of one about "going to see those faraway places with the strange-sounding names" and looking for "those castles in Spain" when we were too bothersome. He died at 46 and never got to take those trips, but he was often on my mind, when my mother and I traveled to some of those places.

During the school year if we were home, my sister and I were put on watch duty to give Mother a heads-up as soon as we spied Dad walking down the street. If we were off somewhere when he arrived, his voice would boom around the neighborhood and we would come running. It was dinnertime and he had earned his evening meal.

• CAROL SUPLICKI

person important in my life. My husband Frank will have to forgive me but I shall write about my father as the person most important in my life. Unfortunately I was separated from my parents for 9 years. When, after Kristallnacht, we finally realized that we had to leave Germany. To get someone out of the concentration camp in our case Buchenwald, we had to promise we would leave Germany within a short time period. My mother went to Berlin and bought visas for Argentina. But my parents ended up in Bolivia. As a young girl at that time, I knew they would marry me off. Since I had a boyfriend from home, who was in the U.S.A at that time, I chose not to go with my parents but went to England on a Domestic permit, in do transport was till the age of 16 and I was 17 at that time. So I was

The Shoe and the Grove

I knew of the great hall,
    the Names set in the wide floor,
illuminated by the flickering lamps:
    Dachau, Bergen-Belsen, Buchenwald, Treblinka –
and the documents and photographs recording
    with characteristic thoroughness the events from
the Nuremburg Laws onward:
    The Yellow Stars, the grotesque caricatures in the
children's books, Kristallnacht and all that followed –
    the jammed-full rail cars, the families lined up, waiting
to be selected for labor or for death, the ZYKLON-B
    canisters, the ovens, the mounds of barely fleshed skeletons.
And, the staring, starving, surviving remnant . . .
    Near the end was a glass case containing a single child's
Shoe, plucked from the debris at Auschwitz, with a
    placard, recording the number included in the
FINAL SOLUTION –
    We went out, a coldness of despair in my heart and
mind, untouched by the bright Jerusalem sun. Then, a
    grove of small trees, each marked with a name –
Danish, Dutch, French, Polish, German, Italian and more, the
    names of the Righteous who aided, comforted and
concealed the prey of the SS and Gestapo –
    I thought of the Righteous during the dark endless years
of the German occupation, living with hundreds of willing
    helpers of the Nazi murderers, and with thousands who
wanted only to survive, eyes shut to the oven smoke,
    ears and hearts closed to the cries of the slaughtered –
and they, fearing the early morning fist at the door, and
    too often, hearing it.

I marveled at the Righteous, and felt the coldness
    lift a trifle,
as we read every name in the Grove,
    while the bus waited . . .

- MIKE ROSEMAN
  Israel 1976

Proof of Living

My husband Frank will have to forgive me, but I shall here document my father as the person most important in my life.

My father was a modest person with many gifts. As young man, he won many dueling contests, and I still remember the sword he proudly kept. But he was a gentle father. On Sundays he and I would go to the post office and he would lift me up to gather the mail from our box. Then we would feed the ducks at a nearby brook. When my cousins and I were children, he wrote plays that we performed for the grown-ups at parties, and he wrote the most beautiful love poems for my mother. I have fond memories of traveling with him to the old cemeteries in the Harz Mountains to gather information for the book he published about the Jews in Nordhausen for the town's one thousand year anniversary.

All this ended with Hitler.

My father was a lawyer. First he was no longer permitted to be a notary, then permitted only to represent Jews. Since our town had only 100 Jewish families and three Jewish lawyers, he had to let the office staff go. My uncle gave him work in his clothing factory, and we gave up our large apartment to move in with my grandfather.

I was separated from my parents for nine years when, after Kristallnacht, we finally realized that we had to leave Germany. My mother went to Berlin and bought visas for Argentina. At 17 years old, I knew they would marry me off and went instead to England on a Domestic Permit, where I worked first as a maid and then in the defense industry.

My parents escaped to Bolivia, and in 1945 were given permission to enter the United States, but could not afford the trip. Relatives sent them the money to come to Baltimore. My father found an ad in a Jewish paper from a china factory in Trenton, New Jersey. Both my parents got jobs there; my father painted the dolls and my mother did repair work.

When the American soldiers returned at the end of the war, my parents lost their jobs and returned to Baltimore. Like many refugees, my father became a Fuller Brush man, traveling on the bus with all his brooms and brushes. My father had a delicate stomach all his life and lost to stomach cancer at the age of 67, too soon, alas, to have met my sons.

My father's book survived the war. Hidden by neighbors when all books by Jews were confiscated, it has since been reprinted by the mayor of Nordhausen. And like my father, I became a translator and notary, helping immigrants to tell their stories and enabling survivors entitled to reparations to document their Proof of Living.

I still think of my father every day.

• EVA SLONITZ

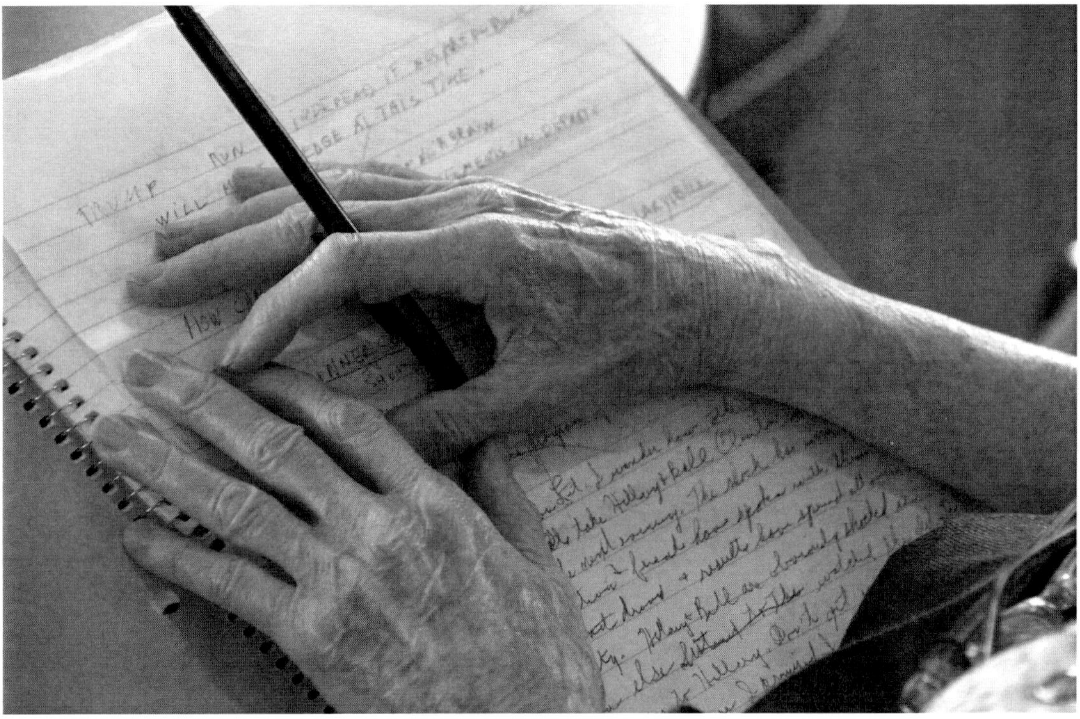

To Anne

How worthy of praise, her qualities gleam
no longer, in person, can we on her gaze
her sterling attributes take life in my dreams
together we shared some glorious days.

Obstacles encountered, she kept her calm
no crisis provoked a mood of alarm
she always succeeded in finding the balm
that comforted pain and lessened the harm.

From her abilities the family gratefully derived
practical remedies that somehow she knew
no special studies were needed to thrive
and accomplish the goals that she kept in view.

Fond memories, I hold, of my wonderful wife
her guidance, still with me, brings meaning to my life.

• JOSHUA ROSEMAN

*If I may be so bold,
Let's stop writing about being old.*

LEE RUBIN

Redefinition

A Perfect Day

A perfect day begins with a prayer of gratitude that I am alive! Yes I made it again and I can smell the air and see the sun or clouds or hear the chirps of birds outside my home.

As the hours pass, I taste ambrosia; come what may, I am grateful again.

- LORRAINE GELULA

In My Dreams

In my dreams, I am still quite young
but then I wake, and feel a hundred and one.

Just yesterday, it seems, I tucked my children into bed,
today, I spied gray hairs on their heads.

I'm not the same as I was, I have no doubt,
where I used to go in, I now go out.

My back is all achy, they replaced my knee,
my parts are different than they used to be.

Age has dulled my every ability,
I have little strength, not much agility.

Age is a state of mind? Baloney, I say,
I'll take youth or middle age any old day.

Still, though I may not be all that I used to be,
I am content. Today's good enough for me.

• BEVERLY SHARE

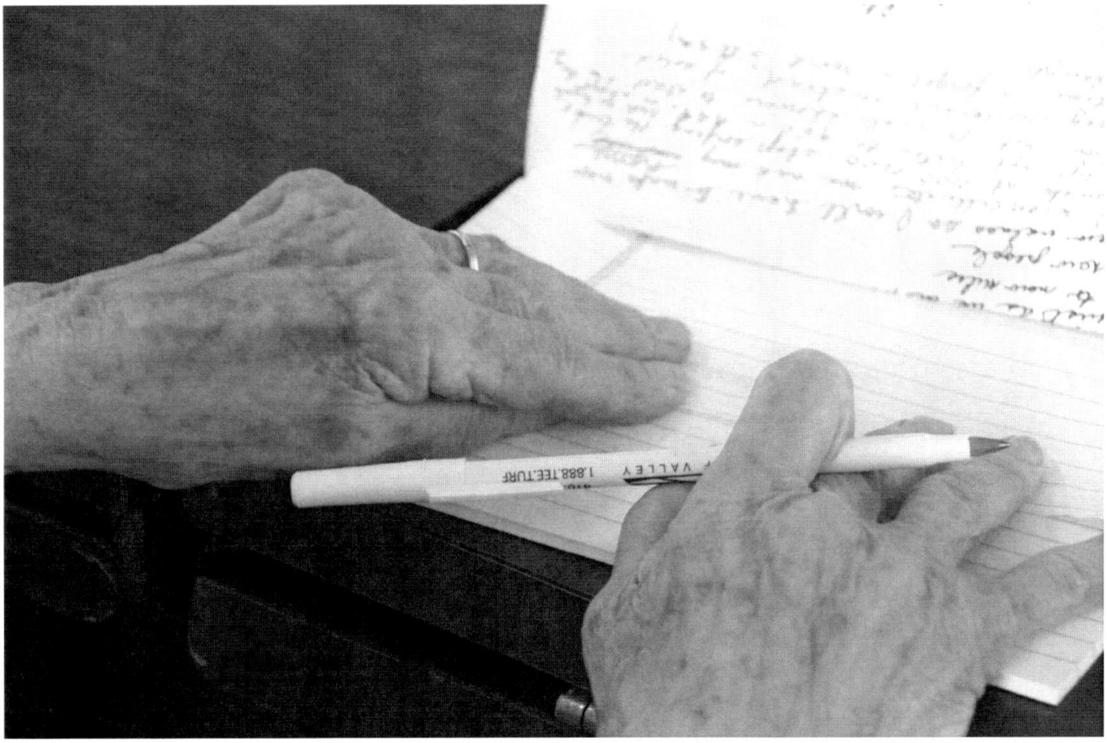
VALLEY
1.888.TEE.TURF

You Never Wrote Me a Shakespearean Verse

You never wrote me a Shakespearean verse.
You never painted my portrait à la Warhol or da Vinci.
Each tortured rhyme got a little bit worse;
each sketch you drew made my face look pinchy.

You can't write poems like Edgar Allan Poe
or spin romantic tales like Sir Walter Scott
or paint a sunlit field like Vincent Van Gogh
or probe the psyche like T. S. Eliot.

But a teasing glance from your wicked eyes
can raise my temperature 'til I blush.
How have you become so wise
to speak my heart with no language between us?

You own my life, my soul, my heart;
you are the master of love's art.

- CAROL SUPLICKI

A New Decree
reflections on graduation

To this golden land, in ships they arrived.
Hardship and tyranny, they had survived.

The immigrants worked very hard to succeed.
To assure that their families would not be in need.

Children's education was their main mandate,
as sacred as the eleventh commandment.

And, following the directive, the children became
professionals and experts, degrees to their name.

The parents, also, should share some of the glory.
Listen and I'll continue the story . . .

They never marched in graduation processions,
too busy battling economic depressions.

No Latin letters follow their names,
but they've earned our praise, just the same.

They perservered and labored, with all their heart
so that their children could get a good start.

So, I say, Graduates, set up a decree,
our parents are worthy of a degree.

Its title should not baffle ye.
They are Masters of Humanity.

• JOSHUA ROSEMAN

nificant in my white attire.

A few years later, I was delighted I had marched the convention Hall aisle to the beat of Pomp and Circumstance with George when I picked up the Atlantic City Press and read that he had been killed on D day! my friend, my hero.

To this day, I wonder whether it is George, D day, or Pomp and Circumstance that creates that feeling of nostalgia in me.

Pomp and Circumstance

I wonder if everyone who has graduated from high school or college has the feeling of nostalgia that grips me whenever I hear the strain of "Pomp and Circumstance."

As I prepared to leave the girls' exit at the Atlantic City Convention Hall, I heard the massive organ thundering the famous melody. I felt insignificant in my white robe and cap but nonetheless eager to see who my male partner would be as he emerged from the boy's exit. Happily it was my friend since 7th grade, George Garber. I was glad to share that happy experience with him rather than a fellow I did not like.

George looked unusually handsome in his blue gown and cap.

I tried to look forward and not guess where my parents might be sitting. Finally our class was all seated and the organ hushed. Speeches began and awards were given. I turned my head and spied my beaming parents. I felt proud, no longer insignificant in my white attire.

A few years later, I picked up the *Atlantic City Press* and read that George had been killed on D-Day. My friend, my hero.

To this day, I wonder whether it is George, D-Day, or "Pomp and Circumstance" that creates that feeling of nostalgia in me.

- LORRAINE GELULA

The Ideal Music Shop

In the early 1920s when my parents were first married, they opened a store on Gay Street in East Baltimore, where they sold player pianos, Victrolas, and phonograph records. It was probably Mother who came up with that original name, The Ideal Music Shop.

At that time, many of the store's customers were Italian and naturally loved Italian opera. Some of them were bricklayers, stone masons, and even street cleaners who found the money to buy a Victrola, plus weekly purchases of those expensive Red Seal Victor opera records, including such favorites as the sextet from *Lucia di Lamermoor* and arias from *Rigoletto*. As Mother said, "They put bread on our table."

My parents lived in a dark apartment upstairs from the store. They soon had a baby, a girl, who they named Lola.

Mother, who had been working as a salesperson in the store, came downstairs while Baby Lola was napping and waited on customers. It wasn't easy. And then – oops – when Lola was only six months old, she became pregnant with me. Yet she continued to help Dad in the store both as a bookkeeper and salesperson.

Now, was it possible for me – still in her womb – to actually hear that sextet and those *Rigoletto* arias, those best sellers that, as Mother said, "put bread on our table?" It happens that, whenever I hear those arias, I begin to hum along as if I know them well, and even had heard them long ago. Long, long ago ... maybe even before I was born!

As the 1920s drew to a close, The Ideal Music Shop went through several changes. First, when the radio was the hottest thing on the market, Dad was the first merchant on Gay Street who featured it in his store. The player pianos soon became obsolete and were no longer taking up space. The Victrolas remained, though replaced by electric phonograph players. There was also an updated record department with popular songs, gospel, blues, country music, along with some opera favorites.

In the early 1930s, Dad began selling appliances such as refrigerators and washing machines, and then the poor little Ideal Music Shop began to look like a health center.

After WWII, the name of the store was changed when it became part of our larger family business that originally belonged to my maternal grandfather, Louis Mazor. It was simply Mazor's, where Dad sold cheap furniture, as the discount houses had control of both TV and home appliances.

Yet somehow this store, with its new merchandise and new name, was pictured in *The Sun,* with a photo of Martin Luther King Jr. – just one week before he was assassinated – speaking to crowds gathered in front of the old Ideal Music Shop.

- HILDA PERL GOODWIN

Following Edward Roseman

Dad was born in Baltimore in 1898, the third of eight children born to my Russian immigrant grandparents. The family lived in a rowhouse on East Baltimore Street, opposite Patterson Park. Edward was a bright boy who loved reading. He attended night school, learned accounting and obtained a CPA certificate, worked in accounting, and then became an entrepreneur, always his own boss. In 1922, aged 24, he wed Anna, then 22, a wonderful wife and mother, and a great help to him. I was born in 1926, my sister Rita in 1934. Dad was a fine father, humorous and always stressing the importance of telling the truth and keeping promises. In the early 1930s, Dad and a partner formed a new business, packaging rubbing alcohol, mineral oil, and other non-prescription sundries. He hired the necessary help and provided his acute business sense, ambition, confidence and fine character.

Dad voted for FDR the first time and against him the other three, to the dismay of his brothers and sisters. When I was 12, I asked him why, and he replied that the president was too involved in laws and rules affecting businesses, especially small ones. One day while visiting in Washington, we neared the White House, and I said, "Slow down, Dad, so I can boo out the window." He, in a stern voice said,

"YOU WILL **NOT.**

THE PRESIDENT OF THE UNITED STATES LIVES THERE AND YOU'LL SHOW RESPECT FOR THE OFFICE, EVEN IF YOU DISAGREE WITH THE MAN!"

That quieted me.

Time passed, and in 1946, out of the service, I enrolled in the University of Maryland and met my future wife, the beautiful Bernice. A year later when my father lost his partner, I left college and joined Dad's office. At his suggestion, I followed in his footsteps, went to night school, and eventually got my CPA certificate. As Bernice and I raised our two daughters, I helped Dad and learned much about business from him.

My father, since childhood, would occasionally stammer, something his family and friends were very accustomed to. A local car dealer broadcast a demeaning TV ad that showed a fast-talking salesman convincing a stuttering customer. Dad wrote a calm letter to the dealer, pointing out that their ad money would be more effective if it did not feature a medical condition from which many people suffered. A week later he received a reply from the ad agency saying he was right. They were pulling the ad and would he be interested in writing copy for them? Dad accepted the apology but declined the job offer, saying that he had decided to stay with his own pharmaceutical firm.

Sadly, during an August night in 1957, my father passed away in his sleep at the age of 59, mourned by all, an example to me, forever. In 1961 I sold the firm to a pharmaceutical company near the harbor, and went along as a manager. That company, in turn, was resold to a Midwest corporation that decided to combine our operation with a West Baltimore plant. I got a call from them one morning telling me to gather the employees, to tell them the operation would be moving, and to fire dozens of employees that very day. I protested — *This is inhumane! People deserve proper notice!* — but to no avail. I did what was ordered, and I was ashamed. My dad would not have done this.

A decade later, in 1973, the CEO called to tell me that the Baltimore operation had been sold and would be closed down and transferred to Tennessee in stages over several months. "Don't tell anyone now," he said. "They'll all exit at once to get new jobs." I refused, saying, "I'll not lie to my people. I'll call a meeting today, advise the people of the gradual shutdown, assure them of fair treatment, and thank them for their past and future cooperation. I'll prepare references for each one and will help them find other work. If the owners don't agree, replace me now!" They reluctantly agreed; I held my meeting, and as I expected, the move went well. In June 1973 I turned in the company car, feeling Dad's smile.

• MIKE ROSEMAN

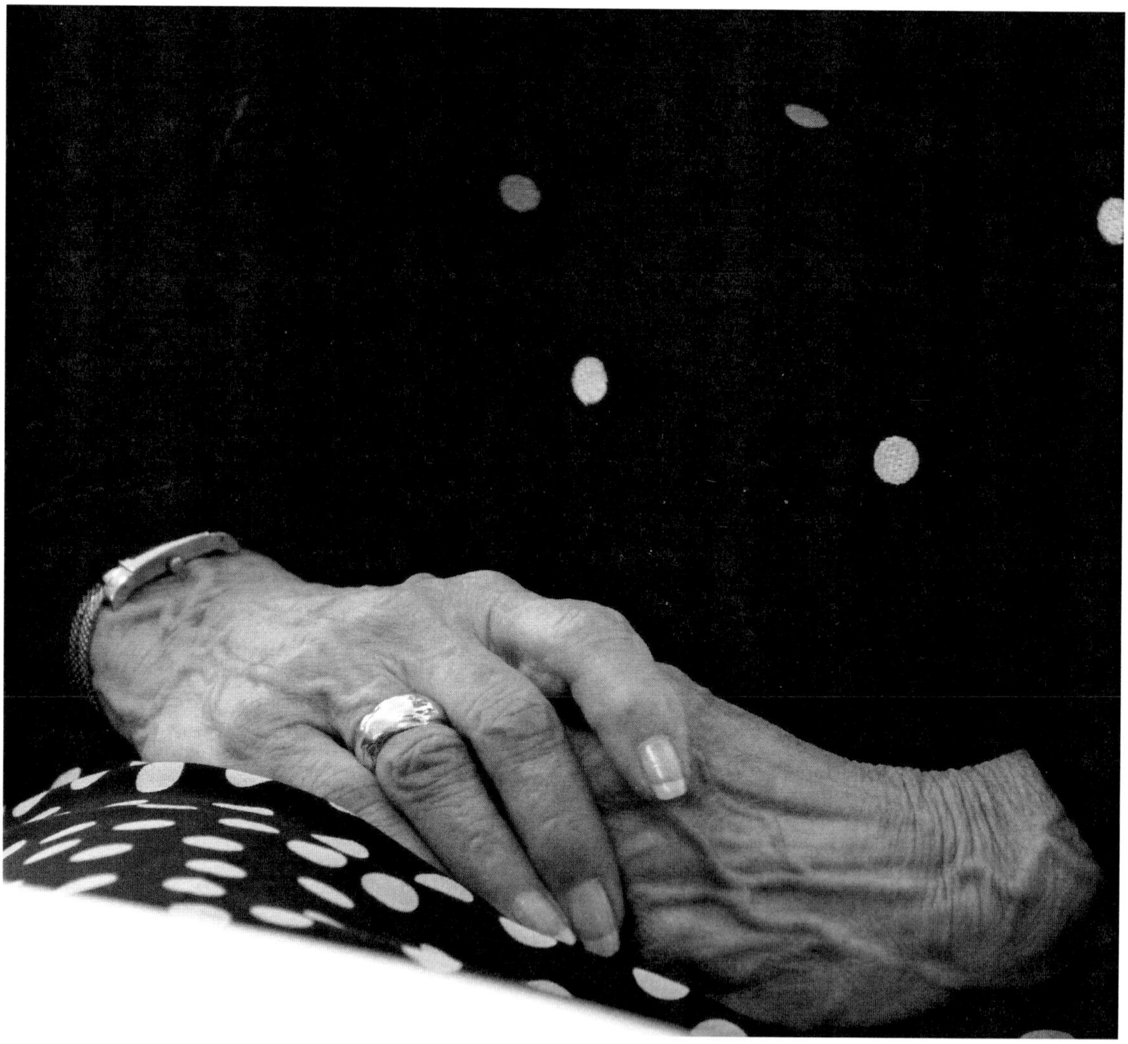

Ode to My Dad's Violin

Last night I enjoyed the most memorable recorded concert I ever heard. Each appearance stood out and each performer was spectacular, but most unforgettable was a young Chinese violinist. She played "Meditation from Thais," and a number of other very familiar beautiful compositions, which I remembered my father going around the house playing from memory. When I was a young child he played for a symphony orchestra and later for himself. He lost his heart and soul in his playing – as she did – and I was suddenly carried back.

How well I recall my dad's recollections of his struggles to become a fine classical violinist. He was the next-to-eldest of five handsome brothers in an immigrant Latvian family from the area of Minsk. His ambition was not appreciated by a maternal uncle, who deliberately broke his fiddle in the family's attic where my father practiced; that had been the last straw for him, and he left, at age 13, to make his way in New York City among many other great talents. He lived chiefly on bananas and milk in those days, he said, and roomed with other musicians who later became famous, including Radio City Orchestra Conductor and virtuoso Erno Rapee, who once borrowed my father's overcoat and pawned it. It was tough for young musicians to survive those early years on their own. My dad studied with great musicians from whom he won scholarships and gold medals; I still have two from celebrated Henry Schradieck and Walter Damrosch.

But this is an ode to the handmade old German violin he had once found in a pawnshop, which he immediately recognized as special and cherished ever after.

Dad's fiddle had a rich, silken tone elicited from its wonderful hand-carved wood scrolls on either side of its delicate light bridge. Its piercing reverberations and deep range were magnificent. Its use is now shared by my son Neil and his older son Alex, and I trust it may go down through the family as something we all respect because of dear Dad.

Dad expected me to become the next Maude Adams and I got my first violin when I was four years old. It was like a beautiful toy and I got a music lesson from Dad almost every day. We moved to Delaware when I was five years old, on Dad's doctor's advice to lead a less harried and pressured life. His older sister, who lived in the Eastern Shore area, conspired with my mother to move us to Harrington, Delaware. It was a completely different lifestyle experience for all of us, but we adjusted.

Among the new people we later met were relatives of the Baltimore Blausteins, who were very interested in good classical music. They later invited my father to come play for them at their home in tiny Ridgely, Maryland. I remember that my father took me along, as he often did; sometimes I played my violin too. We also were invited to entertain at ladies' Century Club meetings annually in nearby towns. My father began driving me 200 miles a week for violin lessons from Herman Weinberg, one of his former co-workers in the Philadelphia Orchestra.

One cellist who visited us was also an academic psychology professor at the University of Pennsylvania. He once spent much time trying to prepare me and my parents to not expect me to continue to get superior grades at Goucher College, where the level of competition would be much higher than in Harrington. I believed him – but happily fared well.

My serious connection with music ended with Goucher. I took my violin freshman semester but brought it home at Christmas, and never took it back. My "excuse" was that it wasn't fair to the other girls in the dorm for me to practice while they were trying to study. I'm sure my dad was very disappointed at the time, but I left little chance to discuss it; I was very busy socially as well as academically, and I know he was very fond of Len, my future husband, and vice versa. I have few regrets.

- MARGIE WARRES

A Sense of Gratitude

Until I moved to North Oaks, I never knew or envisioned being limited in my navigation. Though I am still driving, I now know that we shall never again take long, big trips, which we have loved each year until settling here.

It is a resignation to what must be – nationally as well as globally. Yet there is a sense of gratitude for the past adventures, the wonderful experiences, for all that we have seen and done, for plans carried out with foresight, accomplishments not fully completed, but nevertheless satisfying.

- MARGIE WARRES

Courage

I remember the thrill as my very beautiful newborn son was presented to me in the army hospital of the First Division in Macon, Georgia, where we were stationed. But then he was not seen again for days. Why? A shocking congenital handicap of one leg, which would lead to many lengthy orthopedic visits throughout his early years.

When Steve was perhaps five years old, wonderful Dr. Nachlas determined that only the surgical removal of his entire left foot would ease his discomfort. I suppose we all looked forward to improvement in his everyday life, but not to the surgery itself. It was done at Sinai Hospital in the morning, with just my husband Len, Steve and me present and hopeful. While Steve was in recovery, Len and I went to lunch.

When we returned, a handsome little boy greeted us with a warm smile and said, "I'm doing very well."

We returned the grin, but asked, "How do you know?"

He said, "I dialed Information and asked them how Steve Warres was doing, and that's what they told me."

Len and I chuckled at the resourcefulness of this little tyke, who would later go on to dance in Park School musical productions, climb mountains while serving in the Peace Corps, help countless patients as a psychiatrist, and become a grandfather, himself.

We followed Steve's example, and we, too, dialed Information. Soon after, we dared to have a second child, now also a psychiatrist and grandfather. Steve and Neil remain great buddies to this day.

- MARGIE WARRES

On My Way to Tomorrow

Before I can lay myself to rest, I need to sum up my pluses. Often I am aware of my minuses – they yell to me, unlike my pluses that just whimper. So I'm going to try a new technique.

> First Rule: Don't exaggerate.
> Second Rule: No pity parties.
> Third Rule: Limit the time this exertion will last. Ten minutes, no more.

How shall I evaluate myself so far? Not bad. I'm on my way to tomorrow. Not bad.

• JUDY MICHELSON

The Top of the Stairway

I can't believe I'm here. Shall I just stay here and dwell on what an accomplishment it is to have reached this peak? I must be close to something ahead, and I certainly don't want to go back down. What do I do now? Look ahead. Meditate. There must be another future for me.

The top of the stairway could mean the start of something good. Perhaps another good life, with love and happiness all around. So much can come if we think in an optimistic way. Can that be? That there could be another wonderful life if we dared to think it could be wonderful?

When you're at the top, you don't need to climb. You pause. You gaze. You breathe in, and release a luxurious sigh. You look down and realize you see the ground clearly from here – much more clearly than when you were standing on it. You see all the places you have ever visited: cities and countries and continents. You are not alone. You hold hands. Sometimes you sing.

- **THE WRITING GROUP**

Depends on What the Weather Brings

Spring is the nervous season,
the trees near blown away by wild winds,
then caressed by sun-softened breezes.

New-made sap pumps through tree trunks
to reach the budding leaves and flowers.

The summer solstice encourages
exuberant spurts of growth;
the trees fill out their canopies,
gap-toothed from winter's winds and storms.

The heat pours down during
the long hours of the long days;
the rich greens of the leaves go dull
and the roots probe deep for water.

The dog days of August bark out their warning,
and the trees produce seeds and fruits
in such profusion that they feed a multitude
and still fill a forest with new trees.

Fall trees along the road are bare,
except for some, too fond,
their limbs clasping drooping leaves,
forgetting, for now, how to let them fly –
then partnering with the wind
in the dance that lasts till spring.

If the winter is not cruel,
Spring leaves will pop
and clothe the trees in summer green.

Redefinition

Winter does not surprise the trees,
their food factories already shut down,
turning leaves gold or red or brown.

Their trunks, branches, and twigs,
stripped bare for winter's work,
stretch out against the ice-chilled sky.

It's time for the internal artistry
that records their growth in annual rings —

some wide, some narrow;
it depends on what the weather brings.

• CAROL SUPLICKI

The North Oaks Writers

Howard Joseph Cohen

I grew up in an observant Jewish family in New York and graduated from City College with a bachelor's degree in Chemistry, later earning a master's degree from George Washington University. Several fine chemists mentored me, and, over the years, I was awarded twelve patents for new chemical compounds.

My studies were interrupted when I was drafted into the army. For my service in the Korean War, I was awarded the Presidential Combat Infantry Badge with two Battle Stars. My wife Bernice and I married while I was still in the service and raised two daughters. Today, my main motivation for writing is so that my grandson will know something of his family's history, values and experiences.

Upon retirement I volunteered with the AARP, filing federal and state taxes at a senior center, and with the Maryland Attorney General's Office, responding to consumer complaints. At North Oaks I participate in many activities, from leading Yizkor services, to doing senior aerobics, to gardening. Committing memories to paper is satisfying, and I've found the writing workshop a source of comfort, camaraderie, and – when we occasionally get it just right – comic relief.

Lorraine Gelula

My brother and I grew up in Atlantic City, where my father owned a grocery store and butcher shop. My mother died when I was very young, but I was very fortunate to be brought up by my second mother whom I loved dearly. One of my granddaughters is named after her.

Music was a big part of our lives, and my brother went on to become an operatic singer. After helping my father in the grocery store throughout high school, I went on to secretarial school.

My husband and I had a full life. He ran a jewelry store, and together we had three sons, ten grandchildren and eighteen great-grandchildren. I've been a lifelong member of Hadassah and founded the North Oaks chapter. My children tell me that among my legacies to them are my excellent brownies, the essays I required them to write about events and vacations that made them the good writers they are today, and the love of family that made them feel as if even those relatives no longer living were in the room with them.

I moved to North Oaks in 2002. For many years I had the privilege of chairing the Hospitality Committee and being among the very first to welcome newcomers to their new home and community here.

Hilda Perl Goodwin

My grandparents arrived from Eastern Europe in 1892. I was born in 1922, a second generation Jewish American. I was the second of Blanche and Samuel Fivel's three children, a near twin to my older sister Lola, with a much younger brother. I was blessed to grow up with educated parents and close ties to my extended family.

My father owned a store called "The Ideal Music Shop," where he sold Victrolas, phonograph records, and player pianos. There, as I picked out tunes on the player piano at age three, my lifelong passion for music was born.

I was married to Morris Perl in 1941, while I was still a student at Goucher College. After serving in the army, Morris worked as a furniture factory representative, and I stayed home with our two children, now Mary Azrael, passager editor, and Dr. Edward Perl. After our children entered school, I resumed my studies at Peabody Institute, earned a master's, and began teaching music privately and in the public schools. Sadly, Morris died of multiple myeloma in 1980 at age 61.

In 1984, I married Douglas Goodwin and we had 25 happy years together, travelling, enjoying concerts and plays, and sailing. I offered continuing education courses and presented and produced classical music programs for the Gordon Trust.

Throughout the years, I have been a member of Baltimore Hebrew Congregation, where I have studied Torah and Hebrew, and sung in the congregational choir.

I began a new life at North Oaks in 2013, where I have made new friends and stay involved in music and writing, with the choir and the writing group.

Hilde Gundel

I was born in Boppard, a little town on the Rhine in Germany, where I attended a Catholic School and had many non-Jewish friends. By the time I was eight, in 1934, I would come home crying because I was no longer included in parties. My best friend and I would secretly climb the fence separating our gardens, but feared being discovered by her older brother, a big shot in the local Hitler Youth.

My parents learned of an English family that would take in three ten-year-old girls, and I was soon on a train from Boppard to Cologne to Holland to England. For the rest of my life I will remember my father, who was always so cheerful, crying like a baby when he said goodbye. I was one of the lucky ones; many of the Jews in Boppard were deported and never returned.

In England, I attended private school, was included in weekend trips to my guardian family's country home, and, at age 14, left school to work in the family's factory as part of the war effort. My parents finally escaped Germany by way of Spain, and in 1944, I was reunited with them in New York City.

On Decoration (Memorial) Day of 1946, I took the subway to meet a group of friends at the Riis Park beach. There I met Hans, who arranged for his original date to take the subway home, while he drove me. We married a year later on Decoration Day, 1947. I have especially good memories of Hans playing his saxophone at parties in the backyard.

I have two daughters (our son died when he was very young) and one granddaughter. I love to take walks and be outside. My life at North Oaks is busy with friends, bridge, canasta, Bingo, music, and writing.

Judy Michelson

I was born in Baltimore in 1935 – the middle of the Depression – to a mother from Russia and a father from Palestine. Their only common language was Yiddish, so that was the language we spoke at home.

My parents had a small grocery store in a depressed area near the harbor. I attended a local elementary school where I was often tormented. The children, many of whom had recently arrived from Appalachia, would accuse me of being responsible for "their Lord's crucifixion," which I vehemently denied to no avail. In middle school I attended School #49, an accelerated school, where for the first time I met students who were academically ambitious, but most of whom lived far from my own neighborhood.

For high school, I traveled an hour and a half by bus to attend Forest Park, with its diverse student body. What a joy! I found friends and decided that I would next attend Sinai Hospital's Nursing School. It was affordable, and living in the dorms gave me an opportunity to socialize with like-minded students. As I grew professionally, I appreciated the respect I garnered and continued to advance my education and career.

I married and raised four children who are now generous, dependable citizens, involved in many ways in the Baltimore community. There have been some bumps in my life, as in others', but I keep picking myself up and going on.

Joshua Roseman

I've had a long life, with rich memories from every decade from the Roaring Twenties onward.

Growing up, vocational guidance in high school was not much in evidence, so we really guided ourselves. Without a driving ambition or imagined talent in a particular area, I embarked on the academic course. Later, I decided to get commercial training as well, eventually earning degrees in accounting and law.

I obtained a federal government job at Fort Meade, Maryland, which was interrupted by the outbreak of WWII. After my service, I was employed in private industry in various accounting positions, but yearned for something more satisfying. I learned that personalities and politics affect both government and private endeavors: conflicts can arise, bosses can be insufferable, programs can precipitously be cut. At the last possible moment, I accepted a position at the Social Security Administration, and my life turned around. The position was fulfilling, and I was able to utilize my education and experience. I retired in 1985 after 18 years of meaningful service.

My wife Anne and I had three children, one whom we lost at just 13 months. The family now includes four grandchildren and seven great-grandchildren. The family ties are close, and to this day we gather together every year for vacation and fun.

At North Oaks, where my brother Morris also lives, I enjoy conviviality with friends, aerobics, painting, the choir, and – of course – the writing workshop, where poetry, like a good friend, provides challenge, insight, and delightful entertainment.

Mishel (Mike) Roseman

I was born in 1926, and my first home was the apartment my parents rented on Auchentoroly Terrace, across from Druid Hill Park in Baltimore. Both my parents were avid readers who encouraged my studies. Being smaller than most of my friends, I didn't play ball as much, preferring a new library book. I graduated high school in 1943 at age 17, enrolled at Johns Hopkins, and then served in the army for two years, all stateside. In 1946 I attended the University of Maryland where I met my future wife Bernice (Bunny). My career spanned working with my father and continuing to run his business after his passing, earning a CPA certificate, and then working with a savings and loan operation from 1972 to 1989. The last – and most rewarding – 20 years of my "career" were devoted to work as a volunteer driver for Jewish Family Services, where I often found myself in the role of companion and witness to such memorable events as the Oath of Allegiance Ceremony, which transforms an immigrant into a United States citizen. Bunny and I have two daughters, five grandchildren, and three great-grandchildren, who are the stars of our lives. Our two daughters, Ellen (a retired social worker) and Marcia (a speech pathologist) now advise us; just as years ago we advised them.

Lee Rubin

The only girl in a family of six brothers, I was born and raised in East Baltimore among other immigrant families from Eastern Europe. Our home language was Yiddish, and our family was Orthodox, strictly observing the Sabbath and all the other Jewish holidays. I attended public school in my neighborhood, and Hebrew school after public school each day, receiving a good Hebrew education that continues to this day to enrich my life.

Money was scarce in our large family, so at Patterson High School, I took commercial courses to prepare for a job immediately after graduation. I went to work as a secretary for the government at the Holabird Army Depot.

I married Julius Rubin, and together we had three children. When they were older I resumed my career with the government, working for over 20 years at the Social Security Administration, also earning a degree in Business and Management from the University of Maryland.

After retirement I became involved in music, and joined my husband, playing with the Baltimore and Takoma Mandolin Orchestras. Some of our happiest days were the times we traveled and performed with the orchestra.

Now a recent resident of North Oaks, I enjoy painting, sculpture, reading, and staying fit.

Beverly Share

I was born in Baltimore City in 1930. My parents owned a grocery store, and above it was a small apartment where we all lived – Mom, Dad, big brother Dave, Zadie and Bubbie, and me. It sounds a bit crowded... and it was. But we managed just fine. It was a multi-everything neighborhood. The Black church was just up the street, and my closest friends were Polish twins, Jessie and Marie Garonski. After my grandparents died, we moved uptown to an actual house.

Even as a young girl, writing was an important part of my life. I would spend hours reading Nancy Drew mysteries and writing my own short stories. As an adult, I held a variety of positions – as secretary and salesperson, in real estate and at a retail boutique – but primarily in education in Baltimore County. Working with learning-disabled children was the most challenging work of my career, and also the most rewarding. The best part of my life? A long, loving marriage, and raising a daughter and a son.

After the death of my husband I moved to North Oaks and am enjoying a variety of activities here. As always, writing is at the top of the list.

Edith Sherr

I was born, raised and educated in New York City. I married Martin Sherr, who was also born, raised, and educated in New York City. We both worked fulfilling and productive careers – he, an engineer, and I, a teacher – and I am proud to say I've taught one thousand people how to read. After retiring from the classroom, I enjoyed a fascinating and challenging part-time career doing high school guidance and placement. Looking back, though, my happiest years were the ones I was a stay-at-home mom raising Barbara, who is now this writing workshop's instructor.

In the fall of 2005 I reluctantly stopped working when we made the difficult decision to move to Baltimore to be near Barbara and her family. It was not easy leaving our friends, the theatres we enjoyed, the museums we frequented, the restaurants we savored, the city we loved.

We came to North Oaks, and in a very short time felt at home, made friends, and became involved in the life of the community. After two years Marty died, and I realized I had to make a choice: be sad and lonely or craft a new life as a widow. I chose the latter.

I became interested in the purpose and responsibilities of the Residents' Association, and was elected to serve in various capacities on the Executive Committee, including four years as President. I take pride in knowing that, with the aid and good counsel of so many others, my dedicated service to the community has made North Oaks a better and stronger community for all residents, present and future.

Eva Slonitz

I was born in Nordhausen, a small city in the center of Germany surrounded by the Harz Mountains. My grandfather was a prominent physician and president of our Reform congregation, my father an attorney, and my mother an English instructor. I enjoyed school and enjoyed writing, but by the time I was 15, the Nazis were in power and Jews were no longer allowed to attend school.

My parents fled to Bolivia, but I was hoping instead to reach America, where my boyfriend from Nordhausen was living. The only way to escape Germany at the time was to get to England as a domestic, so I found myself in London working for Mrs. Usher, a widow who was running her late husband's sawdust factory. Interestingly, the Nazis respected my grandfather and never touched him.

The war effort was urgent, so I next learned to operate a lathe in a machine shop. Frank was an expert machinist who mentored me, then married me. We moved to the U.S. and had two sons.

For many years I worked with immigrants in Baltimore, as a notary and translator for the American Red Cross. I would often visit North Oaks to help survivors provide the "proof of living" that would enable them to receive reparations from Germany.

I am fortunate now to live here, with so many kind neighbors and good friends.

Carol Suplicki

I am a child of the Depression, so I learned to value work and to enjoy life without spending a lot of money. I am a child of WWII, so I learned to value my country's founding principles and to honor the sacrifices they demand. And I am a child of the Western canon, from Biblical stories through the Greek plays, to the great works of English and American literature. These influences make me a stoic, a romantic, a naturalist, and a realist. I always enjoyed writing as well as reading, and earned a B.A. in English at Muhlenberg College in Pennsylvania.

When I was choosing a career, room-sized computers were just becoming necessary tools in the business world. I started as a programmer and progressed through jobs as a systems analyst, technical manager, planner, and computer room designer. During my career, I was writing and training others to write documentation of the work and how it was to be used. These computers have been replaced by the ones that sit on your desk or ride around in your backpack or cuddle in the palm or your hand. I became obsolete.

As my house and I aged together, I started looking for a less demanding living style. After visiting different types of retirement communities, I chose North Oaks and moved here in 2004. I participate in the Activities Committee, the Writing Workshop, and in social events. After eleven years here, I feel right at home.

Margie Warres

At age five, I moved from Philadelphia to the Eastern Shore, where I grew up in bucolic surroundings and graduated as Valedictorian from Harrington High School. I won a summer scholarship to Northwestern, where Jennifer Jones, Patricia Neal, and other stars were classmates and friends.

I entered my still beloved Goucher College in 1936, and married Dr. Leonard Warres in 1940, turning down a full scholarship to Columbia Law School in order to accompany Len to various medical posts before he was shipped overseas among the first combatants in North Africa. I ultimately earned a Master of Social Work degree from the University of Pennsylvania. Len and I had two sons, Steve and Neil, both of whom became psychiatrists – perhaps the outcome of many dinner conversations that routinely crossed medicine and social work.

For 36 years, I had the privilege and pleasure of directing the Central Scholarship Bureau, helping countless deserving students achieve their educational dreams. The Child Study Association, several Medical Auxiliaries, Baltimore Hebrew Congregation and Goucher College all kept me busy as an involved volunteer. Many of my best memories, though, are of world travel, including notable "service trips" to Afghanistan in 1973 with Care Medico, and later to Nepal, and Peru, long before these became popular tourist destinations.

Although it has been some time since I've been abroad or ridden a horse, I continue to stay busy and enjoy writing, music, exercise, the stimulation of new ideas, and my sons and their outstanding wives, five grandchildren and two great-grandchildren.

Marty Waxman

In Brooklyn I was born and bred,
The Great Depression making it hard to get ahead.
We walked to school, but home, we'd run
to play ball, make mischief, have some fun.
To make a few bucks, there were always ways,
running errands and bussing tables in those days.
Dropped out of college when a chance came my way,
as copy boy on a New York paper, known as J-A.
Then college basketball scandals opened the door
to sports reporter, my dream job, work I adored.

But the Korean War had begun
and I was among the drafted ones
deployed not to Korea but to Germany
to serve in the Signal Corps, luckily.
Returning to the paper after the two required years,
I found a country gripped by McCarthyism fears
aided by Journal American owner Hearst.
No place for integrity, so out I burst.
Unemployment was no match for our marriage made in heaven,
producing three great kids and grandchildren seven.
With my dream job of sports writer packed up and gone,
I went off to heal the world, tikkun olam.
Ten years union-organizing and public relations
then 25 serving Jews in Baltimore, Israel, and oppressive nations.
But raising funds and representing our much-admired community
was a labor of love and presented the opportunity
to engage with living legends: Ben Gurion, Israel's first premiere,
Dayan, Eban, Rabin, Peres and Golda Meir.
Then retirement, consulting, travel, shows, babysitting and ball games
A life I could never have imagined in those Brooklyn depression days.

About the Editors

Barbara Sherr Roswell

Barbara teaches writing at Goucher College, where she's directed the Writing Program, founded the Goucher Prison Education Partnership, and developed approaches to teaching that link universities with the communities around them. She is also engaged with a variety of organizations beyond the campus, including North Oaks, where she volunteers with the writing workshop.

Christine Drawl

Christine is a fiction writer and designer, and new to Baltimore. She is working on her M.F.A. in Creative Writing & Publishing Arts at the University of Baltimore, and is the Managing Editor for Passager Books.

IN LEGENDS, the crane stands for longevity, peace, harmony, good fortune and fidelity. A high flyer, it is cherished for its ability to see both heaven and earth.
These ancient, magnificent birds, so crucial in the wild as an "umbrella species," are now endangered and must be protected.

Passager Books is dedicated to making public the passions of a generation vital to our survival.

View from the Hilltop was designed, typeset, photographed and illustrated by Pantea Amin Tofangchi. The text pages are set in Bembo.

Printed in 2015 by Spencer Printing, Honesdale, PA.

Also from Passager Books

A Cartography of Peace
poems by JEAN L. CONNOR

Improvise in the Amen Corner
poems & drawings by LARNELL CUSTIS BUTLER

A Little Breast Music
poems by SHIRLEY J. BREWER

A Hinge of Joy
poems by JEAN L. CONNOR

Everything Is True at Once
poems by BART GALLE

Perris, California
poems by NORMA CHAPMAN

Nightbook
poems by STEVE MATANLE

I Shall Go As I Came
poems by ELLEN KIRVIN DUDIS

Keeping Time:
150 Years of Journal Writing
edited by MARY AZRAEL & KENDRA KOPELKE

Burning Bright:
Passager Celebrates 21 years
edited by MARY AZRAEL & KENDRA KOPELKE

Hot Flash Sonnets
poems by MOIRA EGAN

Beyond Lowu Bridge
memoir by ROY CHENG TSUNG

Because There Is No Return
poems by DIANA ANHALT

Never the Loss of Wings
poems by MARYHELEN SNYDER

The Want Fire
poems by JENNIFER WALLACE